[S.S. 555.]   1a/27231.

Vocabulary

OF

German Military Terms

AND

Abbreviations

FIRESTEP
Editions

General Staff,
    General Headquarters.

April, 1917.

FireStep Editions

FireStep Publishing
Gemini House
136-140 Old Shoreham Road
Brighton
BN3 7BD

www.firesteppublishing.com

First published by the General Staff, War Office 1917.
First published in this format by FireStep Editions,
an imprint of FireStep Publishing, in association with
the National Army Museum, 2013.

NATIONAL
ARMY
MUSEUM
www.nam.ac.uk

ISBN 978-1-908487-66-7

Cover design FireStep Publishing
Typeset by FireStep Publishing
Printed and bound in Great Britain

Please note: *In producing in facsimile from original historical documents, any
imperfections may be reproduced and the quality may be lower than modern
typesetting or cartographic standards.*

(B 8911)   Wt. w. 1693—9716   5M   5/17   H & S   P. 17/79

A.

Abänderung	alteration.
Abbauen	to dismantle (*a wireless station*).
Abbinden	to set (*concrete*).
Abbrechen	to break off ; change from line formation to column formation.
Abbrechen (des Schiessens) ...	to cease fire.
zur Kolonne abbrechen ...	to break into column.
Lager abbrechen	to strike camp.
Abdämmung	blocking (*a trench*).
Abdanken	to discharge, dismiss from the service.
Abdeckerei	knacker's yard.
Abdichtungsring	rubber washer (e.g. *for hermetically closing receptacles in food carriers*).
Abdruck	copy.
Abdrücken	to press the trigger.
Abendmeldung	evening report.
Abfall	slope of a hill ; waste, refuse.
Abfangen	to catch, capture.
Abfangen (ein Telegram) ...	to intercept a telegram.
Abfeuern	to discharge, fire off.
kernrecht abfeuern ...	to fire point blank.
Abflauen	to decrease, to abate (*artillery fire*).
Abfrage-Apparat	exchange operator's instrument (*telephone*).
Abgabe	discharge (*light signals, &c.*).
die Mannschaften sind in der Abgabe der Leucht-patronen unterrichtet.	
Abgang (zur Truppe, &c.) ...	discharge (from hospital, &c.).
Abgang	departure.
Abgangsfehler	error due to " jump " (*gun, rifle, &c.*).
Abgangsrichtung	line of departure (*of a shot*).
Abgangswinkel	angle of departure (*of a shot*).
Abgeben	to give, to deliver, to transfer (*of soldiers*).
Abgehen	to start off.
Abgesessen !	Dismount !
Abgezweigt (-e Kompagnie) ...	detached (company).
Abhalten	to hold off, restrain, check.
einen Appell abhalten ...	to call the roll.

Abhang	slope ; hill side.
Abhören	to intercept.
eine Unterhaltung abhören	to intercept a conversation.
eine Telegraphenleitung abhören.	to tap a telegraph line.
Abhören	listening, tapping (a message)
Abhörnetz	listening system.
Abhörstromlauf	listening or tapping circuit.
Abhörtätigkeit	listening, tapping.
Abhörverfahren	listening, tapping.
Abkochen	to cook.
unterwegs abkochen	to cook on the march.
Abkommandieren	to detach, detail.
Abkrümmen	to fire off (rifle).
Abkürzen	to abbreviate.
Abladen	to unload ; unloading.
Abladekommando	unloading party.
Ablegen (Gepäck)	to take off (packs).
Ableitungen	leads (electric), short circuits.
Ablenken	to divert (attention).
Ablösen	to relieve.
Ablösung	relief.
die Ablösung geht vor	the relief is in progress.
Ablösungstruppen	relieving troops.
Abmarsch	marching off.
Abmarschiert!	fired ! (colloquial = "abgefeuert")
Abmarschpunkt	starting-point.
Abneigung	a turning aside, divergence; alteration (in range, elevation).
Abort	latrine.
Abprallen	to ricochet.
Abpraller	ricochet.
Abprallweite	length of ricochet.
Abprotzen	to unlimber.
Abrechnen	to deduct, subtract.
50 Meter abrechnen ...	to shorten range 50 metres.
Abrede	agreement ; denial.
Abreissschnur	" pull-out " string.
Abreissvorrichtung	firing device.
Abriegeln	to block.
Abrücken	to move off.
Abrüsten	to disarm, demobilize.
Abrüstung	demobilization ; disarmament.
Absatteln	to unsaddle, " off-saddle."
Abschied	departure.
seinen Abschied erbitten ...	to ask to be placed on the retired list.

seinen Abschied nehmen ...	to resign one's commission, to quit the service.
Abschiessen	to fire off.
Abschlagen	to repulse.
Abschluss	sometimes joint (as in "gasdichter Abschluss" = gas-tight joint).
Abschneiden	to cut off (retreat, &c.); sometimes to coincide.
Abschnitt	sector.
abschnittsweise	by sectors.
Abschrift	copy.
Abschwenken	to wheel (to right or left).
Absender	sender (of a letter, postcard, &c.).
Absendestelle	dispatching point.
Absetzen (das Gewehr) ...	to bring the rifle to the "ready" (after firing).
Absetzen (Seitengewehr) ...	to unfix (bayonets).
Absicht...	intention, view.
Absitzen	to dismount.
Abspannen	to unhook.
Absperrung	barricade, blocking.
Abspriessen	to strut (engineering).
Abstand	distance.
Abstecken	to mark out; to undo, unfasten.
Absteckpfahl	iron peg.
Absteifung	strutting (engineering).
Absteigen	to descend, go down; to dismount.
Abstellen (Motor)	to shunt off (a motor).
Abstellgleise	siding.
Abstreuen	to scatter, sprinkle.
mit Schrapnell abstreuen ...	to sweep with shrapnel.
Abstufen	to form steps, graduate.
Abstürzen	to fall headlong (referring to aeroplanes).
Abstützen	to prop, strut.
Abteilung	detachment, flight, &c., section (of War Ministry, General Staff, &c.); (not translated if it refers to field artillery, when it is a group of 3 batteries).
Abteilungsbefehl	order of artillery "Abteilung."
Abteilung für Licht und Kraft	electrician detachment.
Abteilungskommandeur (artl.)	"Abteilung" commander(artillery).
Abtransport (im)	on the move (from).
Abtreppen (nach)	to form steps (down to) (when excavating).

Abwarten	to wait for; to attend to *or* groom (*horses*).
Abwässerungsanlagen ...	drainage system.
Abwehr	defence.
Abwehren	to repel, ward off.
Abwehrfeuer	defensive fire.
Abwehrgeschütz	anti-aircraft gun; gun for repelling the assault.
Abwehrgraben...	support *or* reserve trench.
Abweichen	to branch off; to avoid.
Abweichung	departure from (*orders*); deflection, deviation.
Abweisen	to repulse, beat back.
Abzäumen	to take off the bridle.
Abzeichen	badge, distinguishing mark.
Abzeichentuch	cloth used for badges.
Abziehen	to take off; to divert; to evacuate.
ein Gewehr abziehen ...	to pull the trigger.
von der Wache abziehen ...	to come off guard.
Abzug	retreat; outlet; trigger.
Abzugsbügel	trigger guard.
Abzugsfeder	trigger spring.
Abzugsgriff	trigger.
Abzugsschleife...	string loop (*on band of hand grenade*).
Abzugsvorrichtung	trigger device.
Abzweig	point of bifurcation (*e.g., of two galleries in mining*).
Abzweigstollen	branch gallery (*mining*).
Achsband	axle clip.
Achsbandhalter	axle guard.
Achse	axle tree.
Achsel	shoulder.
Achselband	aiguillette.
Achselklappe	shoulder strap (*N.C.Os. and men*).
Achselschuppen	metal epaulettes.
Achselstück	shoulder strap (*officers*).
Achsenbruch	breaking of an axle tree.
Achsenzahl	number of axles (*in a train*).
Achsschmierbüchse	tin of axle grease.
Achteck	octagon.
Achtung!	Attention! Look out!
Achtung! Gas!	Look out! gas!
Adjutant	adjutant.
Flügel-Adjutant General-Adjutant } ...	Aide-de-Camp to the Emperor.
Adjutantur	Administrative staff (*not translated—retain*).
Affe	pack (*slang*).

Afla (Artillerie-Flieger-Abteilung).	artillery flight.
Agent	agent, spy.
Aktenkasten	despatch-box.
Aktiv	regular, Active (as opposeu reserve, &c.).
Akofern (Armee-Fernsprech-Kommando).	Army Telephone H.Q.
Akofunk (Armee - Funker-Kommando.	Army Wireless H.Q.
Alarm	alarm.
Alarm blasen	to sound the alarm.
Alarmbereitschaft (erhöhte) ...	(increased) readiness for action.
Alarmbestimmungen	alarm orders.
Alarmpatrone	signal rocket.
Alarmplatz	alarm post, alarm station.
Alarmposten	sentry to give the alarm.
Alarmsammelplatz	assembly post, assembly station.
Alarm schlagen ... ⎱ Alarmsignal geben ... ⎰	to sound the alarm.
Alarmstellung	support line.
Alarmvorrichtungen	appliances, devices for giving the alarm.
Alarmzustand	" Stand to."
Alarmzustand (aufheben) ...	(to give) " Stand down."
Alarmsignale (geblasene) ...	bugle calls, whistles, &c.
Albatros	" Albatros " (a make of aeroplane).
Alder-B-Munition	" Alder B " ammunition (explosive bullet for anti-aircraft purposes).
Allerhöchste Kabinettsordre...	Order of His Majesty in Council.
Allerschwerst	heaviest (calibre).
Allgemeine Wehrpflicht ...	universal military service.
Allgemeines Aufgebot ...	levy en masse.
Älter	senior.
Älterer Unteroffizier	senior N.C.O.
Altmessing	brass scrap.
Altmetall	metal scrap.
Amboss (der Zündglocke) ...	detonator cap (literally, anvil).
Ambossklotz	anvil block.
Ammonal	ammonal.
Amt	office.
Anbinden	to tie to.
mit jemandem anbinden ...	to put in communication (telephonic) with someone.
Anbrechen	to break, dawn.
Anfall	attack.
Anfangsgeschwindigkeit ...	initial or muzzle velocity.
Anfassen	to take hold of, pick up (arms).

Anfertigen	to make, manufacture, construct, prepare.
Anfordern	to demand, request.
Anführen	to lead.
Anfuhr	supply.
Angaben	statements.
Angaben (beglaubigte)	statements (verified).
Angeldraht	trip wire.
Angezeigt	indicated, advisable, expedient ; announced, reported.
Angreifen	to attack.
Angriff	attack.
Ablenkungsangriff	feint attack, diversion.
Gegenangriff	counter-attack.
Hauptangriff	main attack.
einen Angriff liefern ...	to deliver an attack.
Luftangriff	aerial attack.
Scheinangriff	feint attack.
Angriffsabteilung	assaulting party.
Angriffsart	method of attack.
Angriffsbefehl	order to attack, attack orders.
Angriffserfahrungen	experiences in attack (*e.g.*, *of an army*).
Angriffsfeld	zone of attack.
Angriffsfront	front of attack.
Angriffshandlung	conduct of the attack.
Angriffskrieg	offensive war.
Angriffslücke	gap formed to facilitate the attack.
Angriffsplan	plan of attack.
Angriffsstelle	point of attack.
Angriffstempo (in Einklang gebrachtes)	(pre-arranged) time-table of the attack, *literally*—pace of the attack.
Angriffsverfahren, planmässiges.	methodical attack.
Anhalt	guide (*e.g.*, *to construction, conduct, &c.*).
Anhaltspunkte	instructions.
Anhöhe...	high ground, hill, slope.
Ankerrödel	anchor line belaying pin (*bridging*).
Ankertau	cable.
Anklammerungspunkt ...	a " holding on " point, strong point.
Ankündigungskommando ...	cautionary part of a word of command.
Anlage	emplacement, position, arrangement ; appendix (*orders, documents, &c.*).

Bahnanlage	railway buildings, &c.
Festungsanlage	fortifications.
Scheinanlage	dummy trench or work.
Anlauf	rush, advance.
beim ersten Anlauf... ...	at the first onset.
Anlegen	to take aim ; to plan ; to construct.
ein Manöver anlegen ...	to suggest a scheme for manœuvres.
Anleitung	instruction.
Anmarsch	approach.
Anmarschieren	to approach.
Anmarschlinie	line of approach.
Anmarschrichtung	direction of advance.
Anmarschweg	approach, communication trench.
Anmelden, sich	to report one's arrival.
Annähern, sich	to approach.
Annäherungsgraben ... }	communication trench, approach
Annäherungsweg ... }	trench.
Anordnen	to arrange, order.
Anordnungen	arrangements, dispositions.
Anrichten	to produce, cause ; to regulate.
Anrücken	to march up, advance (against).
Anruf	telephone call ; challenge (of a sentry).
Anrufen	to challenge, hail ; to call up (telephone).
Ansagen	to announce, notify.
Anschaffen	to provide, procure.
Anschalter	separator (mining).
Anschaltvorrichtung	tapping device (electrical).
Anschauen	to inspect ; to observe (a position).
Anschirren	to harness.
Anschlag	firing position, the " present."
Anschlagshöhe	height over which a man can fire.
Anschleichen, sich	to creep up to.
Anschliessen, sich	to join up with.
Anschluss	connection, junction (e.g , with other troops) ; enclosure, annexe.
geben Sie mir Anschluss mit	put me through to (telephone).
Anschluss-Batterie	adjoining battery.
Anschluss-Kompagnie (-Zug)	flank company (platoon) ; directing company (platoon).
Anschlussmann	connecting file.
Anschneiden	to cut ; to make intersections ; to obtain a bearing on (e.g., gun flashes).
durch Anschneiden feststellen.	to locate by intersection.

Anschnitt	bearing.
Ansetzen	to launch (e.g., an attack).
Anspannen	to stretch, strain; to hook in horses.
Anspornen	to stimulate.
Anstalt	establishment.
Ansteckmagazin '	detachable magazine.
Anstellung	appointment.
Anstrich	colouring.
Ansturm	assault.
Antenne	the " aerial " (wireless); wireless station.
Antransport (im)	on the move to.
Antreiben	to drive, urge on, set going.
Antreten	to begin.
wir wollen zum Sturm antreten.	we are about to attack.
den Dienst antreten ...	to assume duties.
Anweisen	to direct, point out.
Anweisung	instructions.
Anzeige	notice, announcement.
Anzeigen	to give notice ; to report ; to proclaim.
Anzeiger	marker.
Anzug	suit, dress.
Arbeitsanzug	fatigue dress.
feldmarschmässiger Anzug	marching order.
Apotheker	chemist.
Apparat	apparatus, instrument.
Appell	roll call ; the " assembly " (cavalry).
Appell abhalten	to call the roll.
beim Appell fehlen... ...	to be absent from roll call.
Appellplatz	parade ground.
Arbeit	work, labour.
Arbeitende Mannschaft ...	working parties.
Arbeiterbataillon	labour battalion
Arbeitsabteilung	fatigue party.
Arbeitsdienst	fatigue duty.
Arbeitskommando	fatigue party.
Arbeitskompagnie	labour company.
Arbeitsplan	working plan.
Arbeitssoldat	soldier of a disciplinary corps,
Arbeitstrupp	work squad.
Arbeitsverwendungsfähig ...	fit for labour employment.
Arendt-Gruppe	listening set section
Arm	branch gallery (mining).
Armauflager	elbow rest.

Armbinde	armband, brassard; sling.
Armee-Abteilung	Army Detachment (*equivalent to an Army*).
Armee-Befehl	Army order.
Armee-Bekleidungs-Depot ...	Army clothing depôt.
Armee-Bericht	Army report, bulletin, despatch.
Armee-Fernsprech-Abteilung	Army telephone detachment.
Armeegruppe	Group (*equivalent to a Corps*).
Armeehauptquartier	Army Headquarters.
Armeekorps	Army Corps, Corps.
Armeelastzug	army mechanical transport train.
Armeelieferant	army contractor.
Armee-Musik-Meister ...	Inspector of Military Bands.
Armee-Oberkommando ...	Army Headquarters (*Staff*).
Armee-Post-Direktor ...	Director of Army Postal Services.
Armee-Post-Inspektor ...	Army Postal Inspector.
Armee-Telegraphen-Abteilung	Army telegraph detachment.
Armeeverordnungsblatt ...	Army Orders.
Armeeverwaltungs-Department	Army Administration Department.
Armeezahlmeister	Army paymaster.
Ärmelaufschlag	cuff (*of tunic, &c.*).
Ärmelpatten	sleeve patches.
Armierung	armament.
Armierungsbataillon	labour battalion.
Armierungskabel	armoured cable.
Armstützen	tackle brackets (*bridging*).
Arrest	arrest.
Mittelarrest	light field punishment.
strenger Arrest	close arrest.
Arrestant	man undergoing confinement.
Arrest-Kasten	place of confinement, cell.
Arrest-Lokal	guard room.
Arreststrafe	confinement.
Arrest-Zelle	place of confinement, cell.
Arriere-Garde	rear guard.
Art	pattern (*e.g., alter Art, neuer Art*).
Artillerie	artillery.
Artillerie-Anschneidetrupp ...	artillery survey section.
Artillerie-Depot	ordnance depôt; artillery park.
Artillerie-Entwicklung ...	deployment of artillery.
Artillerie des Feldheeres, schwere.	heavy artillery of the Field Army.
Artillerie-Fernsprechverbindung	artillery telephone communication.
Artillerie-Feuer	artillery fire, bombardment.
Artillerie-Feuer (flankierendes)	enfilade artillery fire.
Artillerie-Flieger-Abteilung ...	artillery flight.
Artillerie-Geschoss	shell, projectile.

Artillerie-Kampf	artillery duel.
Artillerie-Kommandeur ...	artillery commander.
Artillerie-Konstruktionsbureau	Artillery Technical Section (of Technical Institute).
Artillerie-Messtrupp	artillery survey section.
Artillerie - Munitions - Depot (— Lager).	artillery ammunition depôt.
Artillerie-Munitions-Kolonne	artillery ammunition column (heavy).
Artillerie-Nachrichten-Sammelstelle.	artillery information centre.
Artillerie-Prüfungs-Kommission	Ordnance Committee.
Artillerie-Schiessplatz ...	artillery range.
Artillerie-Schiess-Schule ...	School of Gunnery.
Artillerie-Tätigkeit	artillery activity.
Artillerie-Unterstützung ...	artillery support.
Artillerie-Verbindungs-Offizier	artillery liaison officer.
Artillerie-Vergeltung	artillery retaliation.
Artillerie-Werkstatt	artillery workshop.
Arzneikasten	medicine chest.
Arzt	medical officer (for ranks of medical officers, see under " Generalstab-sarzt ").
Aspirant	(usually not translated), Aspirant, candidate.
Assistenzarzt	Second-lieutenant (medical).
Astgabel	rest (e.g., for a rifle).
Astverhau	abatis.
Atemeinsatz	breathing drum (of gas mask).
Atemfilter	breath filter (of gas mask).
Atemsack	respiratory bag.
Atemschützer	respirator (gas).
Atemwiderstandsfeldprüfer ...	resistance gauge for breathing drums (gas).
Attacke	charge.
Attila	hussar tunic.
Auditeur ⎱ Auditor ⎰	Judge-Advocate.
Auditoriat	Judge-Advocate's officials.
Aufbewahrung...	storage.
Aufbrechen	to strike camp ; to start.
Aufenthalt	stop, stay ; beat (of a sentry).
Auffahren	to come into action (of artillery).
Auffangen	to intercept.
Auffordern	to summon, challenge.
Aufforderung	request, order, demand.
Aufforderung zum Schuss ...	request for fire to be opened.
Asto	listening set.

Auffüllung der Gräben mit Truppen.	massing troops in the trenches.
Aufgabe	duty, task (e.g., Aufgabe einer Batterie).
Aufgebot	ban (of Landsturm or Landwehr); calling out of troops.
Aufgebot, allgemeines ...	levy en masse.
Aufhängeriemen	brace.
Aufhau...	breaking out (mining).
Aufheben	to call up ; to withdraw an order.
Aufheben einen Posten ...	to capture a post.
Aufhebungsbezirk	recruiting district.
Aufklärer	scout.
Aufklärung	clearing up, reconnaissance.
Aufklärungspatrouille ...	reconnoitring patrol.
Aufmarsch	forming up, assembly, deployment approach march.
Aufmerksamkeit (erhöhte) ...	(a sharp) look out.
Aufnahme	photograph.
Aufnahme des Geländes ...	survey or mapping ; aeroplane photograph.
Aufpflanzen (Seitengewehr) ...	to fix (bayonets).
Aufprotzen	to limber up.
Aufräumen	to clear (trench, dug-out, &c.).
Aufraümungsarbeit	salvage work, re-opening work
Aufräumungswelle	wave of infantry attack detailed as clearing up parties.
Aufrechterhaltung	maintenance.
Aufreiben	to annihilate.
Aufreibende Märsche ...	exhausting marches.
Aufrichten	to erect ; to drive forward horizontally from bottom of an incline (mining).
Aufrollen	to clear or work along (a trench, &c.).
Aufsatz...	gun sight.
Fernrohraufsatz	telescopic sight.
Libellenaufsatz	clinometer sight.
Aufschlag	burst on impact.
Aufschläge	facings.
Aufschlagsgeschwindigkeit ...	striking velocity.
Aufschlagspunkt	point of impact.
Aufschlagzünder (Az.) ...	percussion fuze.
Aufschneideverfahren ...	" flash spotting," (obtaining inter sections on the bursts of shells or flashes of guns).
Aufsichtshabender	officer or man in charge.
Aufsitzen	to mount (horse).
das Ziel aufsitzen lassen ...	to aim at 6 o'clock on the target.

Aufstellen	to form up, take up a position ; to site (*a gun*).
Aufstellung	order of battle *or* forming up.
Auftrag	duty, order, commission.
Auftrag (im)	" By order," " Signed for " (*above a signature on a document*).
Auftreffsgeschwindigkeit ...	striking velocity.
Auftreffstelle	point of impact.
Auftreffsschicht	bursting course (*roof of dug-out, &c.*).
Auftreten	to appear.
Aufwurf	parapet, mound.
Aufzeichnung	sketch.
Aufzieher	extractor.
Aufzugbrücke	drawbridge.
Augen-angreifende Reizstoffe	lachrymators.
Augen links !	Eyes left !
Augen rechts !...	Eyes right !
Augenmerk zu richten ...	to take care, direct attention.
Augengläser	" goggles."
Augentränen bekommen ...	to lachrymate (*owing to gas*).
Augenverbindung	visual connection.
Ausarbeiten (der Ladekammer)	chambering (*mining*).
Ausbau	consolidation or completion (*of a position*) ; construction, improvement (*of defences*).
Ausbilden	to train.
Ausbildung	training.
Ausbildungslager	instructional camp.
Ausbreiten	to extend.
Ausbruch	a breaking out, outbreak.
Ausdehnen	to extend.
Ausdehnung	extent, extension.
Ausfall	sortie.
Ausfallstufe	sortie step.
Ausfragen	to interrogate.
Ausführung (kartographischer Arbeiten).	(map) reproduction.
Ausführungskommando ...	executive word of command.
Ausgabemagazin	refilling point.
Ausgabestelle	refilling point, ammunition distributing depôt.
Ausgang	exit, entrance.
Ausgangsfront	original front.
Ausgangsgraben	" down " trench.
Ausgebeplatz	refilling point.
Ausgehobener	recruit.

Ausheben	to recruit; to requisition; to construct, dig (*trenches*).
Aushebung	levy, conscription.
Aushebungsbezirk	recruiting district.
Aushöhlung	hollowing out, burrowing.
Auskunftei	intelligence office.
Auslade-Kommissar	detraining inspector.
Ausladen ... ...: ...	to unload, detrain.
Ausladepersonal	detraining personnel.
Ausladeort ... ... } Ausladestelle ... ... }	unloading *or* detraining place.
Ausmustern	to discharge, reject.
Ausquartieren	to change billets.
Ausrauchen	to smoke out.
Ausraümen	to clear out; to evacuate.
Ausrücken	to march out, evacuate.
Ausrückstärke...	marching out strength.
Ausrüsten	to equip.
Ausrüstung	equipment.
Ausrüstung, die gesamte (die volle)	full marching order.
Ausrüstung der grossen Bagage	2nd line transport equipment.
Ausrüstungsgegenstände ...	articles of equipment.
Ausrüstungsstück	article of equipment.
Aussage (Gefangenen-) ...	prisoners' statements.
Ausschachtung	excavation.
Ausschalten	to switch off, disconnect.
Ausscheiden	to retire, withdraw from; to keep separate; to reserve, detail.
Ausscheiden (aus dem Kampfe)	to put out of action.
Ausschirren	to unharness.
Ausschlag	deflection (*magnetic compass*).
Ausschliessen	to lock out; to exclude.
210 schliesst aus, 469 Meldung	" 210 get off the line, 469 is sending a report."
Ausschlüpfen	to slip out, creep forth.
Ausschwärmen	to form a line of skirmishers.
Aussendung	transmission (*wireless, &c.*).
Aussenfort	detached fort.
Aussenposten	advanced post.
Aussenwache	outlying picket.
Aussenwerk	outwork.
ausser Dienst (a.D.)	retired (*of officers*).
Aussetzen	to post (*e.g., an outpost detachment*); to expose.
Ausstatten	to equip, provide with.

Ausstattung	equipment, provisioning.
Aussteifern	to strut (engineering).
Aussteigeplatz	arrival platform.
Ausstellen	to post (*a sentry*).
Austausch	exchange, relief.
Ausweichgraben	support trench.
Ausweichstelle...	passing place (*in trench, light railway, &c.*).
Ausweis	authority, permit ; notice, instructions ; consignment note.
dieser Fernspruch gilt als Ausweis	this telephone conversation serves as authority.
Ausweiskarte	pass, permit.
Auswerfer	ejector.
Auszieher	extractor.
Auszimmerung	timbering of galleries (*mining*).
Auszug	extract (*e.g., from orders*) ; departure.
in einen Auszug bringen ...	to epitomise.
Automobilkorps	Automobile Corps.
Avancieren	to promote.
Avantgarde	advanced guard, vanguard.
Aviatik	"Aviatik" (*a particular make of aeroplane*); aviation.

B.

Backtrog	trough (*sometimes formed into a raft*).
Bäckerei	bakery.
Bagage (Gefechts, Grosse) ...	transport (1st line, 2nd line).
Bagageführer	regimental transport officer.
Bahnanlagen	railway buildings, &c.
Bahnbauten	railway constructional works.
Bahn brechen, sich	to push one's way.
Bahndamm	railway embankment.
Bahnhof	railway station.
Bahnhofskommandantur ...	office of railway station commandant.
Bahnlänge	pitch (*bombing practice*).
Bahnnetz	railway net, system.
Bahnübergang...	level crossing.
Bahnwärter	plate-layer.
Bajonett	bayonet; dog leg in a gallery (*mining*).
mit dem Bajonett beginnen	to commence the dog-legging (*of galleries*).
aufgepflanztes Bajonett ...	fixed bayonet.
mit gefälltem Bajonett ...	with bayonet at the charge.
Bajonettgriff	bayonet hilt.
Bajonetthaft	bayonet stud.
Bajonetthals	} bayonet socket.
Bajonetthülse	
Bajonettring	bayonet clasp.
Bajonettstoss	pointing with the bayonet; bayonet thrust.
Balken	baulk, log.
Balkenbrücke	girder bridge.
Ballon-Abwehr-Kanonen-Zug (B.A.K.Z.).	anti-aircraft section.
Ballonbrandgeschoss	incendiary bullet for use against balloons.
Ballonhülle	envelope of balloon.
Band, weisses	surveyor's tape.
Bandenkrieg	guerilla warfare.
Bank	parapet, bank.
Barake	hut.
Barakenbau	hutting.
Barakenlager	hut camp.

Basis	base.
Bataillon	battalion.
Bereitschafts-Bataillon ...	battalion in support.
Ruhe-Bataillon ...	battalion at rest.
Stellungs-Bataillon	battalion in line.
Bataillonsbureau ...	battalion orderly room.
Bataillonskommandeur	battalion commander.
Bataillonsschreiber ...	orderly room clerk.
Bataillonstambour ...	battalion drummer, drum major.
Batterie	battery.
besetzte Batterie ...	a battery which is occupied.
bespannte Batterie	horsed battery.
fahrende Batterie ...	field (artillery) battery.
gedeckte Batterie ...	concealed battery.
in geöffneter Zugkolonne ...	battery column.
reitende Batterie ...	horse (artillery) battery.
schwimmende Batterie	floating battery.
Batteriechef	battery commander.
Batterieplan	battery board.
Batterietrupp	reconnaissance personnel of field battery (with telescope, flags, directors, telephone).
Bauabteilung	entrenching detachment.
Baudirektion	Works Department.
Baugrube	shaft.
Baukommando ...	working party.
Baukompagnie ...	entrenching company, construction company.
Baulichkeiten	buildings.
Bautrupp	construction squad.
Bauweise	method of building.
Bauwesen (Militär) ...	Military Works Department.
Bayerisch	Bavarian.
Beagid	an inflammable product composed of carbide and other substances, used in acetylene safety lamp.
Beamte...	official.
Bedienungsmannschaften (einer Batterie).	personnel, gun crew.
Befehl	order.
Befehligen	to command a regiment ; to be in command of.
Befehlsausgabe ...	issue of orders.
Befehlsbrücke ...	emergency bridge.
Befehlsempfänger ...	representatives of formations for receiving orders.
Befehlshaber	General Officer Commanding.

Befehlsstand ... ... $\rbrace$ Befehlsstelle	command post.
Befehlsübermittlung ...	transmission of orders.
Befestigung	fortification.
Befestigungsanlagen ...	defences.
Befestigungsarbeit ...	defence work.
Befestigungsbauten ...	defensive works.
Befördern	to promote ; to dispatch.
Beförderung	promotion ; transport.
Beförderung dem Dienstalter nach.	promotion by seniority.
Beförderung ausser der Reihe	promotion by selection.
Beförderungsliste ...	promotion roll.
Beförderungsmittel ...	means of transport.
Befreiung	exemption.
Begegnungsgefecht ...	encounter battle.
Begleitmannschaft ...	escort ; men detailed to assist.
Begleitung	escort.
Begraben	to bury.
Behandlung	treatment, handling.
Behelf	expedient, makeshift, subterfuge.
Behelfsbrücke	temporary bridge.
Behelfskonstruktion ...	makeshift type (e.g., of hand grenade).
Behelfsmässig	improvised.
Behelfsschlitten ...	improvised sledge.
Beherrschen	to rule over, command, overpower, control.
Behörden	authorities.
Feldverwaltungs-Behörden	Field Administrative Authorities.
Beilage	annexe ; enclosure ; appendix.
Beilpicke	pickaxe.
Beinwickel	puttee.
Beitreibung	requisitioning.
Bekämpfen	to engage.
Bekleidung	clothing ; revetting (of a trench).
Bekleidungsabteilung...	Clothing Section of the Intendance.
Bekleidungsamt (B.A.)	clothing office.
Bekleidungsstärke ...	clothing strength.
Bekleidungsstück ...	article of clothing.
Bekleidungsvorschriften	Dress Regulations.
Beköstigung	messing.
Belag	roadway or planking (of a bridge).
Belagern	to besiege.
Belagerung	siege.
Belagerungsarmee ...	besieging army.
Belagerungsartillerie ...	siege artillery.

Belagerungskrieg	siege warfare.
Belagerungs-Park	siege park.
Belagerungs-Telegraphen-Ab- teilung.	siege telegraph detachment.
Belagerungs-Train	siege train.
Beleg	document, proof, voucher.
Belegen	to cover; to occupy ; to shell.
Belegen mit Schnellfeuer ...	to open rapid fire on.,
Belegung	occupation ; imposition, levy.
Belegungsfähigkeit	maximum levy which a town can sustain ; billeting capacity.
Beleuchtungsmittel	illuminating material.
Beleuchtungswagen	searchlight wagon.
Benachrichtigung	informing, transmission of infor- mation.
Benzinvorrat	petrol supply.
Beobachter	observer.
Beobachtung	observation.
Beobachtungslatte	observation pole.
Beobachtungsmittel	means of observation.
Beobachtungsposten ...	look-out man.
Beobachtungsspiegel	periscope.
Beobachtungsstelle ... Beobachtungsstand ... }	observation post.
Beobachtungswagen ...	observation wagon (*field and foot artillery*).
Bereich	zone, area.
ausser Bereich	out of range.
im Schussbereich	within range.
Bereiten	to prepare; to break in (*a horse*).
Bereitlegen	to make ready for use.
Bereitschaft (in)	in readiness, in support.
Bereitschaften	supports.
Bereitschaftsbüchse ... Bereitschaftskapsel ... }	" alert " box (*gas*).
Bereitschaftskompagnie ...	support company.
Bereitschaftsstellung	support line.
Bereitstellungsraum	point of assembly.
Bergehalle (eines Luftschiffes)	airship shed.
Bergeholz	rubbing strake (*pontoon*).
Berghang	hill side.
Bergkompagnie	tunnelling company ; mining com- pany.
Bergmännisch	relating to miners, mining.
Bergstrich	hachuring, hatching (*topog.*).
Bergung	salvage.
Bericht erstatten	to make a report, report.

Berichten	to report.
Berittener Feldjäger	mounted courier.
Berme	berm.
Berührung	contact.
Besatz	braid (on cap, pantaloons, &c.).
Besatzstreifen	cap band.
Besatzung	garrison.
Sicherheits-Besatzung ...	emergency garrison.
Beschaffenheit	nature, character.
Beschiessen	to shell, bombard, fire on.
der Länge nach beschiessen	to enfilade.
Beschotterung	road metal.
Beschlagschmied	farrier (below the " Fahnenschmied in rank).
Beschlagzeug	farrier's tools.
Beseitigen	to neutralize (artillery) ; to remove (obstacles, &c.).
Besichtigung	inspection.
Besiegen	to defeat, conquer.
Bespannungsabteilung ...	draught horse detachment (foot artillery).
Bespannung einer Batterie ...	battery team.
Besprechung	conference (e.g., of officers).
Bestand	supply ; strength (of a regiment).
Bestand (eiserner)	iron ration.
Beständigkeit	stability.
Bestandsaufnahme	inventory.
Bestätigen	to confirm.
Bestätigung	confirmation, sanction.
Besteck	case of instruments (e.g., surgical)
Bestrafen	to punish.
Bestreichen	to sweep (e.g., with artillery fire).
Bestreichung (toter Winkel)...	sweeping (dead ground).
Beteiligen (sich, an)	to participate in.
Beton	concrete.
Betonarbeiten	concrete work.
Betonbau	concrete structure.
Betonbaukompagnie	concrete construction company.
Betoniert	made of concrete.
Betonschicht	apron of concrete.
Betonstärke	thickness in concrete.
Betontrupp	concrete construction section.
Betonunterstand	concrete dug-out.
Betreffend (betr.) ... ... Betreffs (betr.)	} concerning, with reference to.
Betriebsabteilung	traffic department.
Betriebseinheit	traffic unit.

Betriebsgebiet	... ...	traffic district.
Betriebsinspektion	... ...	traffic inspection.
Betriebsmaterial	... ...	rolling-stock.
Betriebsplan ...	... ...	time table (*railway traffic*).
Bettung ...	... ...	platform, bedplate.
Bettungs-staffel	... ...	platform échelon (in mortar battery).
Beunruhigungsfeuer ...	...	harassing *or* disturbing fire.
Beurlauben ...	... ...	to give leave.
Beurlaubtenstand	... ...	officers and men on furloughed lists in peace time, *i.e., officers and men liable to military service who are not actually with the colours.*
Beurlaubter ...	... ...	man absent on leave.
Beute ...	... ...	booty.
Beutezug	... ...	raid.
Bevorstehend ...	... ...	imminent, impending.
Bewachung ...	... ...	guard, guarding.
Bewaffnung ...	... ...	arms, arming, armament.
Bewaldet ...	... ...	wooded.
dicht bewaldet	... ...	closely wooded.
Bewässern ...	... ...	to irrigate.
Beweglichkeit ...	... ...	mobility.
Bewegungskrieg	... ...	open fighting ; field warfare.
in der Bewegung ...	...	on the move.
eine Bewegung ausführen lassen.		to manœuvre.
Bewilligung ...	... ...	approval, concession, grant.
Bewurf ...	... ...	plastering, mortar.
Bezeichnung ...	... ...	designation (*of units*).
Beziehen ...	... ...	to take possession of ; to draw (*rations*).
ein Lager beziehen	...	to pitch camp.
einen Posten beziehen	...	to occupy a post.
die Wache beziehen	...	to mount the guard.
Quartier beziehen ...	...	to go into billets.
Bezirk	...	district.
Bezirkskommando	... ...	District Command.
Bezirksoffizier	... ...	district officer.
Binde	...	bandage ; belt, sash.
Bindeleine ...	... ...	lashing.
Bindestränge ...	... ...	traces.
Biwak	...	bivouac.
Ortsbiwak ...	... ...	close billets.
Biwaksbedürfnisse	... ...	bivouac requisites.
Biwakskommandant ...	...	bivouac commander.

Biwaksplatz	bivouac ground.
Offizier vom Biwaksdienst	officer on bivouac duty.
Blanke Waffen	cold steel.
Blasebalg	bellows.
Blasen	to blow, to sound (*bugle calls*).
Blasverfahren	emission of gas clouds.
Blatt	leaf, sheet ; record.
Blaue Bohnen	bullets (*colloquial*).
Blausäure	prussic acid.
Blech	sheet iron.
Blechbüchse	tin box ; container (*for gas mask*).
Blechflasche	tin water-bottle.
Blechtafel	corrugated iron sheet.
Blechtornister	water-can (*slung like a pack*).
Bleikern	lead core (*of bullet*).
Blende	loophole ; screen.
Blendlaterne	dark lantern.
Blind	blind.
Blind feuern	to fire with blank.
Blindgänger	a " blind."
Blind gehen	to desert.
Blind laden	to load with blank.
Blindschuss	blank cartridge.
Blinkstation	lamp signalling station.
vom Bock fahren	to drive from the box.
Bock	box of a vehicle ; trestle (*bridging*).
Blockhaus	block house (*also used to describe a machine gun emplacement*).
Blosslegen	to expose.
Bluse	jacket, field service jacket (*latest pattern without buttons*).
Bockbein	trestle leg.
Bockbrücke	trestle-bridge.
Bockgerät	trestle gear.
Bockholm	transom.
Bockkeile	wedges.
Bockwagen	trestle wagon.
Bockwinden	block and tackle.
Boden	ground, earth.
Bodenbedeckung	features (*of landscape*).
Bodenfläche	surface of the ground.
Bodenstück	ground sill of a frame (*mining*).
Bodenzünder	base fuze.
Bogenbahn	trajectory.
Bogenschuss	high angle fire.
Bohle	thick plank, board, " duck board."
Bohrloch	bore hole, auger hole.

Bohrmaschine	... ...	boring machine.
Bohrmine	... ...	bored mine (*mining*).
Bohrpatrone	... ...	small cylindrical blasting cartridge used in auger holes, &c.
Bohrschüsse	... ...	shots (*blasting*).
Bohrzange	... ...	bore pincers (*mining*).
Böller	... ...	small mortar.
Bolzen	... ...	bolt.
Bombe	... ...	bomb (*used by aeroplanes*).
Bombensicher	... ...	shell-proof (*against continuous bombardment by 8-in. guns and heavy "Minenwerfer," or single hits by heavier natures*).
Böschung	... ...	slope (*of a trench*).
Bote	... ...	messenger.
Brandbombe	... ...	incendiary bomb.
Brandgeschoss	... ...	} incendiary shell.
Brandgranate	... ...	
Brandloch	... ...	gas escape hole.
Brandlochverschlussplatte	...	escape-hole disc.
Brandmine	... ...	*Minenwerfer* incendiary shell.
Brandrakete	... ...	incendiary rocket.
Brandrohr	... ...	incendiary flare.
Brandsatz	... ...	powder train.
Brandwirkung	... ...	incendiary effect.
Brecheisen	... ...	crowbar.
Brechreizend	... ...	acting as an emetic (*gas shell*).
Brechstange	... ...	crowbar.
Breite (geographische)	...	latitude.
Breitenstreuung	... ...	dispersion, lateral error in shooting.
Bremsflüssigkeit	... ...	liquid for filling recoil buffer.
Bremsschuh	... ...	brake-shoe.
Brenndauer	... ...	duration of burning (*of fuze*).
Brennlänge	... ...	time of burning, *or* setting of fuze.
Brennpunkt	... ...	focus ; point of burst.
Brennzeit	... ...	time of burning (*of fuze*).
Brennzünder (Bz.)	... ...	time fuze.
Bresche	... ...	breach.
Bresche schiessen	... ...	to make a breach.
Brett	... ...	plank ; chess (*bridging*).
Brettern, bekleidet mit	...	revetted with planks.
Bretterschuppe	... ...	wooden shed.
Brettstapelbrücke	... ...	wooden bridge on piles.
Brett-Tafel	... ...	tail board.
Brieftaube	... ...	carrier pigeon.

Brieftauben-Abteilung ...	carrier pigeon detachment.
Brieftaubenschirrmeister ...	carrier pigeon service, staff-serjeant of.
Brieftaubenschlag	carrier pigeon loft.
Brigade	(1) " Brigade " of field artillery = 2 regiments = 12 batteries.
	(2) Brigade of infantry = 2 or 3 regiments.
	(3) Brigade of cavalry = 2 regiments.
Brigadier	Lieutenant-colonel of military police (Prussia) : military policeman (Saxony).
Brillen	spectacles, goggles (*gas mask*).
Brillen mit Cellongläsern ...	goggles with Cellone eyepieces.
Brisante Eigenschaft ...	shattering effect.
Brisanzpulver	high explosive (H.E.).
Brisanzwirkung	high explosive (H.E.) effect.
Bronze-Mörser...	(21 cm.) bronze mortar.
Brotbeutel	haversack.
Brotbeutelband	haversack strap.
Bruchpunkt	re-entrant (*of a trench*).
Bruchteile	fragments ; disconnected portions (*of trench, &c.*).
Brückenleitung	laddered circuit (*electrical*).
Brückenpfeiler	bridge pier.
Brückensteg	footbridge.
Brückentrain	bridging train.
Brückenwage	weighing machine, weigh-bridge.
Brückenwagen	bridge wagon.
Brunnenbaukommando ...	company for sinking and constructing wells.
Brustklappe	plastron (*of lancer's tunic*), breastplate.
Brustpanzer ... ... ⎫ Brustschild ... ... ⎭	breastplate.
Brustwehr	parapet, breastwork.
Buchhalter	bookkeeper.
Büchse	rifle.
Büchsenmacher (*now* = Waffenmeister).	armourer.
Bügel	stirrup ; ring, hoop ; trigger guard.
Bundesrat	Federal Council.
Bürgerlicher Beruf	occupation in civil life.
Bursche	officer's servant.
Burschenzimmer	orderlies' room.
Bussole	compass (*magnetic*).

C.

Cadre	cadre.
Cellon	" Cellone " (a material like celluloid).
Cellongläser	Cellone eyepieces (in goggles of gas mask).
Central	central, exchange (telephone).
Centralnachweisbureau ...	Central Information Bureau.
Cernieren	to invest, besiege, blockade.
Cernierungsheer	investing army, besieging forces.
Charakterisiert	brevet (rank).
Chargen	officers and non-commissioned officers.
Chargenpferd	officer's charger.
Chargierten	officers and non-commissioned officers.
Chaussee	main road, high road.
Chefarzt	Senior Medical Officer.
Chef des Feldeisenbahnwesens	Director of Railways.
Chef des Feldsanitätswesens	Director-General of Medical Services of the Field Army.
Chef des Feldtelegraphenwesens	Director of Signals.
Chef des Generalstabes	Chief of the General Staff.
Chevaulegers	(not translated ; German term retained) Bavarian light cavalry.
Chiffre	cipher.
Chiffreschrift	cipher writing.
Chiffrieren	to encipher.
Chlorgas	chlorine (gas).
Chlorkalke	bleaching powder, chloride of lime.
Chlorkohlenoxyd	phosgene (gas).
Civil (in)	in plain clothes

D.

Dachpappe	roofing felt.
Dachsbau	dug-out (*colloquial*).
Dampfablassschlauch...	condenser tube (*machine gun*).
Darstellung	representation (*topog.*).
Dauer ...	durability, duration.
Dauerbefehle ...	standing orders.
Dauerfleisch	preserved meat.
Dauerlauf	running exercise.
Dauermarsch ...	forced march.
Dauernd untauglich ...	permanently unfit.
Deckbezeichnung	code designation, code name.
Deckblätter	corrigenda, amendments.
Decke ...	cover, blanket ; tarpaulin : roof of a gallery (*mining*); roof of a dugout.
Deckenstärke ...	thickness of cover, strength of cover.
Deckenstück ...	top sill of a frame (*mining*).
Deckname	code name.
Deckplan	wagon cover.
Deckung	cover.
Deckung gegen Sicht	cover from view.
Deckungsgraben	support trench, cover trench.
Deckungslager...	camp protected from view, but not from fire ; concealed camp.
Deckungslinie ...	line of defence.
Deckungsmannschaft	escort ; covering party.
Deckungsmaterial	roofing.
Deckungstruppen	covering party.
Deckwort	code word.
Degen ...	sword (*infantry and engineers*).
Degengefäss ... Degengriff ...	} sword grip.
Degenklinge ...	sword blade.
Degenknauf ... Degenknopf ...	} sword pommel.
Degenkoppel ...	sword belt.
Degenscheide ...	scabbard.
Degenschneide...	sword edge.
Degenspitze ...	sword point.
Degenstoss ...	sword thrust.
Deichsel ...	pole (*of a vehicle*).
Demobilmachung	demobilization.
Demontieren (ein Geschütz)	to disable, cripple (a gun).
Depesche ...	despatch, telegram.

Detonation	detonation.
Detonieren	to detonate.
Dienen	to serve, to be in the army.
von der Pike auf dienen ...	to rise from the ranks.
Dienst	duty, service.
innerer Dienst	routine duty.
Dienstabzeichen	distinguishing mark or badge.
Dienstalter	seniority.
Dienstanweisung	notification to serve.
Dienstanzug	drill order.
Dienstbeschädigung	wounds or injuries contracted on service.
Diensteintritt	entry into the service.
Dienstfähig entlassen ...	discharged as fit.
Dienstgrad	rank.
Dienstleistung	duty.
zur Dienstleistung kommandiert.	temporarily attached for duty.
Dienstlicher Schriftverkehr ...	official correspondence.
Dienstpferd	troop horse.
Dienstpflicht	liability for service.
Dienstraum	office.
Dienstsiegel	official seal.
Dienststempel	official stamp.
Diensttauglich...	fit for service.
Diensttuend	doing duty.
Dienstunfähig ⎱	disabled, non-effective, incapacitated for service.
Dienstuntauglich ⎰ ...	
Dienstunterricht	instruction, drill.
Dienstvorschrift(en)	regulations.
Dienstweg	official channel.
Dienstzeit	period of service.
Dienstzweig	branch of service.
Direktion	Directorate.
Diskushandgranate	disc hand grenade.
Disposition, zur (z.D.) ...	on half pay (of officers).
Distriktoffizier...	district officer of military police.
Division	Division.
Divisionsadjutant	Divisional administrative staff officer.
Divisionsarzt	Assistant Medical Officer with Division.
Divisionsauditeur	Divisional Judge-Advocate.
Divisionsbefehl	Divisional order.
Divisionsbrückentrain ...	Divisional bridging train.
Divisionsgefechtsstand ...	Divisional battle headquarters.
Divisionsintendant	Divisional Intendant.
Divisionspfarrer	Divisional chaplain.
Divisionsstabsquartier ...	DivisionalHeadquarters.

Dolch	dagger.
Dolchmesser	clasp knife.
Doll	thole pin (boat).
Dolmetscher	interpreter.
Doppeldecker	biplane.
Doppelferngläser	binoculars.
Doppelfernrohr	binocular telescope.
Doppelgeleise	double track (railway).
Doppelkolonne	column of subsections (artillery and machine guns).
Doppelläufig	double-barrelled.
Doppelleitung	double circuit ; metallic circuit.
Doppelposten	double sentry post.
Doppelsterne	lights showing a double star.
Doppelzünder (Dz.)	time and percussion fuze.
Dornbalken	" pin " baulks.
Drachenballon	kite balloon (sausage-shaped).
Dragoner	dragoon.
Dragoner-Regiment	dragoon regiment.
Draht	wire.
blanker Draht	bare wire (electrical).
Drahteinzäunung	wire fence.
Drahtgeflecht	wire netting.
Drahtgeschütz...	wire gun.
Drahtgitter	wire netting.
Drahthindernis	" wire," wire entanglement.
Drahtleitung	wire, lead (electrical).
Drahtlose Telegraphie ...	wireless telegraphy.
Drahtnägel	wire nails.
Drahtnetz	wire entanglement.
Drahtrollen	wire cylinders (of entanglements).
Drahtschere	wire-cutter, wire shears.
Drahtscherertrupp	wire-cutting squad.
Drahtschlinge	wire loop.
Drahtseil	wire rope.
Drahtverhau	" wire," wire entanglement.
Drahtwalzenhindernis ...	cylinder of wire (for entanglements).
Drahtzange	wire nippers, pliers.
Drahtzaun	wire fence.
Drall	twist of rifling (gun or rifle).
gleichbleibender Drall ...	uniform twist.
zunehmender Drall... ...	increasing twist.
Draufgehen	to advance.
Drehbank	lathe.
Drehbolzen	pivot bolt.
Drehbrücke	swing bridge.
Drehen	to turn, to wheel.

Drehung	rotation, turn, twist.
Drehscheibe	turn table (*on railway*), traversing plate (*of trench mortar*).
Dreieckpunkt	triangulation station.
Dreifuss	tripod.
Dreifusslafette...	tripod mounting.
Dreischichteneinsatz	3-layer drum (*for gas mask*).
Dressieren	to train, break in.
Drilchanzug	canvas clothing.
Drillich *or* Drilch	canvas, drill.
Drohen	to threaten, be imminent.
Dröhnen	to boom.
Druckarbeiten	printing work.
Druckpumpe	force pump.
Drückeberger	malingerer ; shirker.
Drücker	trigger.
Durchbrechen	to break through, penetrate, pierce.
eine Blockade durchbrechen	to run a blockade.
strategischer Durchbruch ...	strategical penetration.
Durchbruch	breaking through, penetration.
Durchdringen	to penetrate, force one's way through.
Durchführen	to accomplish, carry out.
einen Angriff durchführen...	to drive home an attack.
Durchführung (einer Belagerung).	prosecution (of a siege).
Durchgang	gangway ; passage, thoroughfare.
Durchgangsschein	permit.
Durchgebildet	experienced, well trained.
Durchlassposten	examination post.
Durchlaufender Erdaufwurf ...	continuous parapet.
Durchlaufendes Drahthindernis.	continuous wire entanglement.
Durchlöchern	to riddle with bullets.
Durchmesser	diameter.
Durchschiessen	to cut by fire.
Durchschlag	carbon copy.
Durchschlag	breaking into the enemy's gallery (*mining*).
Durchschlagen	to penetrate.
Durchschneiden	to cut through, intersect.
Durchschnitt	average.
Durchschnittszeichnung ...	sectional sketch.
Durchstoss	breaking through, inroad.
Durchstossung	bayonet wound, wound caused by a stab or thrust.
Durchwaten	to ford, wade through.
Dynamit	dynamite.

E.

Eben	even, level.
Ebene	plain (*subst.*).
Ebnen	to make level, flatten (*artillery bombardment*).
Eckbalken	corner post.
Eckbrett	bracket.
Eckhölzer	squared timber.
Ecksäule	corner pillar.
Egge	harrow ; also a plank with nails driven and projecting through it used as an obstacle.
Ehrenbezeugungen	military compliments (*e.g.*, *saluting*).
Eichenspreitzen	oak stays.
Eierhandgranate	" Egg " hand grenade.
Eile	hurry.
Eilig	urgent.
Eilmarsch	forced march.
Einarbeiten	to acquaint oneself thoroughly with.
Einarbeiten, gegenseitiges ...	mutual acquaintance with each other's methods.
Einbau	digging in, mounting.
Einbauen (der Batterien) ...	digging in (of batteries).
Einbauten	structures in field fortification (*e.g.*, *shelters, O.Ps., &c.*).
Einbautrupp	working party for constructing emplacements.
Einbrechen	to invade.
Einbruch	raid, breaking in, penetration, invasion.
Einbruchstelle...	point of entry (*of a raid*).
Eindecker	monoplane.
Eindeckung	overhead cover, recess.
Eindeckungen (fortlaufende)	continuous recesses (*under parapet*).
Eindringen	to break into, penetrate, enter.
Einfall	collapse ; invasion ; idea striking one's mind.
Einfallen	to fall in ; to invade:
Einfallswinkel	angle of descent.
Einfordern	to call in ; to demand.
Eingedeckt (schusssicher) ...	in shell-proof emplacement.

Eingedeckt werden	to be covered in, *or* completely "blinded" (*trench, or other works*).
Eingraben (sich)	to dig oneself in.
Eingreifen	to come into action.
Einheit	unit; unity.
Einheits-geschoss	universal or combined (H. E. and shrapnel) shell.
Einimpfen	to inoculate, to inject (*serum*).
Einjährig-Freiwilliger ...	one-year volunteer.
Einkehlen	to groove; to provide with a gutter.
Einleben	to become thoroughly acquainted with (*e.g., a new position*).
Einleiten einen Angriff ...	to prepare an attack ; to begin an attack.
Einmessen	to fix (*e.g., battery aiming points*).
Einmündung	entrance (*e.g., where a communication trench enters a fire trench*).
Einnehmen	to occupy, conquer.
Einquartieren	to billet, quarter troops.
Einrichten	to erect, organize, arrange, settle, prepare.
Einrichtung	arrangement, order.
nach Einrichtung der neuen Stellen.	after the installation of the new stations.
Einrücken	moving in (*e.g., of troops into billets*) ; to be called up (*of recruits*).
Einsatz	bringing up, employment, bringing into action, engagement ; breathing drum of gas mask (*in which case it is a contraction for "Atemeinsatz"*).
Munitionseinsatz	expenditure of ammunition.
Einschalten	to switch on (*electrical*); to insert (*a unit between other units in line*).
Einschärfen	to inculcate.
Einschichteneinsatz ...	single layer drum (*for gas mask*).
Einschiessen, sich ...	to register, begin registration, find the range.
Einschiessensverfahren ...	registration.
Einschiffen	to embark.
Einschlagen	to strike (*of projectiles*).
Einschlagsknall	report of a shell burst.
Einschliessen	to comprise, include.
Einschliessung...	investment (*fortress*).
Einschneiden	to dig in.
Einschnitt	emplacement, embrasure.
Einschraubzünder	fuze (*which is screwed in*).

Einsetzen	to introduce, insert; to put in (*e.g.*, *troops into the line, into the fight, &c.*), engage.
am Apparat eingesetzt ...	engaged at the telephone (*colloquial*).
Artilleriefeuer einsetzen ...	open fire with artillery.
Einspannen	to hook in (*horses*).
Einspringender (Winkel) ...	re-entrant (angle).
Einspritzen	to inject.
Einsteigbrücke	gangway (*for entraining purposes*), ramp.
Einstellen	to put in ; to suspend.
Feuer einstellen	to cease fire.
ein Pferd einstellen ...	to stable a horse.
Rekruten einstellen ...	to enlist recruits.
einen Stollen einstellen ...	to stop a gallery (*mining*).
in einen Truppenteil eingestellt werden.	to be posted to an unit.
sich wieder einstellen ...	to return.
Einstellung	recruiting, enlistment ; suspension.
zeitweilige Einstellung ...	temporary suspension ; intermission.
Einsturz	collapse, fall, downfall.
Einsturz eines Schachtes ...	caving in of a shaft.
Einteilen	to divide into, detail.
Einteilung	division, graduation, disposition ; " order of battle."
Eintreten	to enter, to join the army.
Einverleibt	absorbed.
Einvernehmen	understanding.
Einweiser	guide (*into the trenches*).
Einzelaufzählung	detailed enumeration.
Einzelfeuer	independent fire.
Einzelheiten	details.
Einzelscharte	ordinary loophole.
Einzelschuss	single round.
Einzeltreffer	single direct hit.
Einziehen	to withdraw.
Einzug	entry (*of troops into a town, &c.*).
Eisenbahnarbeiterkompagnie	railway labour company.
Eisenbahnbaukompagnie ...	railway construction company.
Eisenbahnbetriebsamt ...	railway traffic office.
Eisenbahnbetriebskompagnie	railway traffic company.
Eisenbahndamm	railway embankment.
Eisenbahndurchschnitt ...	cutting.
Eisenbahnnetz	network of railways, railwa system.

Eisenbahnschienen	rails.
Eisenbahnschwellen	sleepers.
Eisenbahntruppen	railway troops.
Eisenbeton	reinforced concrete.
Eisenbetonkuppel	reinforced concrete cupola.
Eisenbewehrung	reinforcement (ferro-concrete).
Eisenblechrahmen	sheet-iron frame.
Eisendraht	iron wire.
Eisenflechtung	reinforcement (ferro-concrete).
Eisenklammer	dogs (in timber work).
Eisenklingeln	metallic noise.
Eisenmeissel	iron chisel.
Eisenpfahl	iron stake, post.
Eisenpfosten	iron post.
Eisenplatte	iron plate.
Eisenstange	iron rod.
Eisenteile	iron or metal parts.
Eisenträger	iron girder.
Eiserner Bestand	iron ration (also used in connection with artillery ammunition).
Eiserne Portion	iron ration.
Eisernes Kreuz (E.K.) ...	Iron Cross.
Eisnägel	frost nails.
Elektrikertrupp	electrician detachment.
Elemente (unklare)	suspects.
Elevationswinkel	elevation of a gun.
Ellbogenfühlung	close touch.
Empfangsabteilung	reception detachment (of main dressing station).
Empfangsbescheinigung ...	receipt voucher.
Empfangsstelle	receiving station.
Endstation	terminus.
Engländerwache	guard for British prisoners of war.
Engpass	pass, defile.
Engquartier	close billets.
Ente	" dud " shell (colloquial).
Entblössen	to lay bare ; to expose (a wing).
Entfalten	to deploy.
Entfaltung	deployment.
Entfernung	distance, range.
Entfernung aus der Armee ...	expulsion from the army.
Entfernungsmesser	telemeter, range finder.
Entfernungsschätzer	range taker.
Entgegengehen	to go to meet, encounter.
Entgehen, einem	to escape one's notice ; to lose ; to miss.
Entkommen	to escape.

Entladen	... to unload, discharge.
Entlausen	... to disinfect, rid of vermin.
Entlausungsstube ...	... disinfecting room.
Entlüfter	... suction pump for extracting bad air from a mine.
Entsatz	... relief.
Entsatzarmee	... relieving army.
Entsatzmannschaft ...	... relief-column.
Entscheidung	... decision.
Entscheidungskampf ... Entscheidungsschlacht ...	...} decisive battle.
Entschlammen ...	... to free from mud.
Entsetzen (eine Festung)	... to relieve, succour (a fortress).
Entseuchen	... to disinfect.
Entsprechend	... suitable, corresponding.
Entstänkerungspatrone	... deodorising cartridge (*for getting rid of gas*).
Entwaffnen	... to disarm.
Entwässerungsanlagen	... drainage arrangements.
Entwässerungsgraben	... draining trench.
Entweichen	... to escape.
Entwicklung	... deployment, extension; development.
Entwurf	... draft (*of document*), rough sketch, project, provisional edition (*text-books, regulations, &c.*).
Entziehen	... to withdraw, screen (*from view, fire, &c.*).
Entziffern	... to decipher.
Entzünden	... to inflame, light.
Epauletten	... epaulettes.
Equitations-Anstalt ...	... School of Equitation (Bavaria).
Erbeuten	... to secure, capture (*booty*).
Erdarbeit	... digging.
Erdaufwurf	... heap of earth, mound.
Erdaufwurf (durchlaufender)	continuous parapet.
Erden	... earths (*telephone, &c.*).
Erdkabel	... buried cable.
Erdleitung	... earth, earth line.
Erdmörser	... earth mortar, buried trench mortar.
Erdoberfläche	... surface of the ground.
Erdpolster	... cushion of earth.
Erdsappe (flüchtige) ...	... flying sap.
Erdstation	... ground station.
Erdtelegraph	... power buzzer (*telegraphy*).
Erdvorlage	... layer of earth (*in front of concrete wall, &c.*).

Erfahrungen	experiences.
Erfahrungsgemäss	as a result of experience.
Erfordern	to demand, request, ask for.
Erforderlich	requisite.
Erfordernis	requirement.
Erfüllen	to observe, fulfil.
Ergänzend	supplementary, completing.
Ergänzung	complement; recruiting.
Ergänzungsbedarf	deficiency.
Ergänzungsmannschaften ...	drafts.
Ergänzungsplanquadrat ...	supplementary squaring of a map.
Ergänzungszug	supplementary section (*applied to extra machine gun units formed in* 1916. *The term is now obsolete*).
Ergeben (sich)	to surrender.
Ergebnis	occurrence; result, consequence, sequel.
Ergreifen	to seize, take up (*arms*).
Erhebung	elevation, rising ground.
Erhebungen und Falten ...	undulating ground.
Erhöhen	to increase.
Erhöhung	elevation, height, hill, commanding point.
Erhöhungswinkel	angle of elevation.
Erkennen	to recognise.
Erkennungsmarke	identity disc.
Erkennungswort	watchword, countersign.
Erkennungszeichen	distinguishing mark.
Erklärung	declaration.
Erkunden	to examine, reconnoitre.
Erkundung	reconnaissance.
Erkundungsabteilung ...	reconnoitring party.
Erkundungsergebnisse ...	results of reconnaissance.
Erkundungspatrouille ...	reconnoitring patrol.
Erkundigen, sich nach ...	to inquire after.
Erkundigung	inquiry.
Erkundigungsabteilung ...	reconnoitring detachment.
Erkundigungskommando ... Erkundigungspatrouille ...	} reconnaissance patrol.
Erlass	order.
kriegsministerieller Erlass...	War Ministry order.
einen Befehl erlassen ...	to issue, publish an order.
Erlaubnisschein	permit.
Erläuternd	inquiries being made (*found at the bottom of messages*).
Erläuterung	explanation.
Erledigungsschein	receipt.
Erleiden	to suffer.

Ermächtigung	...	...	authorization.
Ermitteln	... ...	...	to ascertain, determine.
Ernte ...	... ...	...	harvest.
Erntekompagnie		... ...	harvesting company.
Eröffnen (Feuer)		... ...	to open (fire).
Eröffnung	...	... ...	opening.
Ersatz ...	... ...	...	"Ersatz," supplement, reinforce-ment, draft, depôt; substitute.

The word "Ersatz," when used alone means "draft" or "reinforcement." When prefixed to the title of a unit, e.g., "Ersatz Battalion," it either means "depôt" or "supplementary unit formed by a depôt."

(See also "Ersatz Reserve.")

Ersatzbehörden		...	recruiting authorities.
Ersatzgestellung		... ...	substitute, replacement.
Ersatzgläser ...	...	...	spare mirrors (for periscope).
Ersatzkompagnie		... ...	depôt company, "Ersatz" company.
Ersatzmagazin		... ...	reserve depôt.
Ersatzmannschaften ...		...	drafts.
Ersatzmittel ...	...	...	spare parts (telephone, &c.).
Ersatzreserve ...	...	...	"Ersatz Reserve" (category of men surplus to the annual contingent required for the Army in peace).
Ersatzreservist	...	...	"Ersatz" reservist.
Ersatzstollen ...	...	...	substitute (alternative) gallery (mining).
Ersatzstücke ...	...	...	spare parts.
Ersatztruppen	...	...	depôt troops.
Ersatztruppenteil	...	...	depôt unit.
Erschiessen	... ...	...	to shoot dead, execute.
Erschütterungshalbmesser	...		radius of rupture (mining).
Erstatten (Bericht)	...	...	to make a report.
Ersticken (im Keim) ...		...	to nip (in the bud).
Erstickendes Gas	...	...	suffocating or asphyxiating gas.
Erstrecken, sich		...	to extend (e.g., "das Feuer erstreckte sich bis zum rechten Kompagnie-abschnitt"=the fire extended as far as, &c.).
Erstürmen	...	...	to take by assault.
Erstürmung	...	...	assault.
Erweis ...	...	...	proof, demonstration.
Erwiderungsfeuer	...	...	retaliation fire.
Erzwingen	...	...	to force, gain by force.
Eskadron	...	...	squadron.
Eskadronskolonne	...	...	squadron column.
Etappen	...	...	Lines of Communication (L. of C.).

Etappenanfangsort	Home base.
Etappenarzt	Deputy Director of Medical Services (L. of C.).
Etappendelegierter	Delegate for the L. of C.
Etappendepotmagazin ...	depôt on L. of C.
Etappen-Eisenbahn-Direktion	L. of C. railway directorate.
Etappen-Fernsprech-Depôt ...	L. of C. telephone depôt.
Etappen-Flug-Park	L. of C. aviation park.
Etappenfuhrparkkolonne ...	L. of C. supply park.
Etappengebiet...	L. of C. area.
Etappen-Hauptort	L. of C. main depôt.
Etappenhilfsbäckereiabteilung	L. of C. auxiliary bakery detachment.
Etappen-Kommandantur ...	L. of C. Commandant's office.
Etappen-Lazarett	L. of C. stationary hospital.
Etappenmagazin	depôt on L. of C.
Etappen-Ort	post on L. of C.
Etappen-Sammelkompagnie...	L. of C. collecting company.
Etappen-Sanitäts-Depot ...	advanced depôt of medical stores.
Etappen - Telegraphen - Direktion	L. of C. telegraph directorate.
Etat (niederer, höherer) ...	establishment (higher, lower); budget.
Etatsmässig	on the establishment.
Exerzieren	to drill.
Exerziermarsch	drill step.
Exerziermässig	as if it were a drill.
Exerzierreglement	drill book.
Exerzierpatrone	dummy cartridge.
Exerzierplatz	drill ground.
Explosionsmotor	internal combustion engine.
Exzellenz	Excellency (*title given to Lieut.-Generals and senior ranks in the German Army*).

F.

Fabrik	factory.
Fabrikleitung	factory management.
Fach	compartment (*in a box*); branch, department; trade, profession.
Facharbeiter	technical worker.
Fachleute	specialists.
Fachwerkbrücke	truss bridge.
Fähnrich	aspirant officer (second stage), ensign.
Fähnrichsprüfung	ensigns' examination (*of cadets before posting as ensign, &c.*).
Fahne	flag, colours, standard.
Fahne, auf Dienst bei der ...	on active service.
Fahnenflucht	desertion.
Fahnenflüchtiger	deserter.
Fahnenjunker	aspirant officer (first stage).
Fahnenschmied	farrier.
Fahrbar	practicable for wheeled traffic.
Fahrbündel	float (*for improvised floating bridge*).
Fähre	ferry.
Fahrdisposition	time table (*railway*).
Fahrende Batterie	field artillery battery.
Fahrer	driver.
Fahrrad	bicycle.
Fahrtanweis	time table (*railway*).
Fahrtliste	
Fahrtnummer	number given to draft of reinforcements.
Fahr- und Marsch-Tafeln ...	tables of railway movements and marches.
Fahrzeug	vehicle.
Fällen	to fell.
das Bajonett fällen... ...	to bring the bayonet to the charge.
Fallbrücke	drawbridge.
Fallschirm	parachute.
Fallschirmrakete	parachute light.
Fallwinkel	angle of descent.
Faltboot	collapsible boat.
Faltbootbrücke	bridge of collapsible boats.
Falte	fold, hollow.
Falten (Erhebungen und) ...	undulations.
Falzartiger Halter	grooved charger *or* strip (*magazine rifle*).

Fangschnur	cap lines, busby lines.
Faschine	fascine.
Faschinenbekleidung ...	fascine revetment.
Fassen	to hold, to seize (*slang for* "*beziehen,*" *to draw rations*).
Fassung	loading space, holding capacity (*railway*).
Fassungsvermögen	holding capacity (*dug-outs, &c.*).
Faustriemen	sword-knot.
Fechten	to fight, fence.
Federspannung	tension of spring (*in machine gun, &c.*).
Fehlanzeige	nil report.
Fehlen	to miss, err ; to lack.
Fehler	fault, mistake, miss.
Fehlerhaft	faulty.
Fehlgehen	to miss one's way.
Fehlschlagen	to miscarry.
Fehltritt	false step.
Fehlwurf	misfire (*especially applicable to* "*Lanz-*" *or* "*Wurf-Mine*").
Feile	file (*tool*).
Feind	enemy.
Feindlich	hostile, the enemy's.
Feld	field ; land (*of rifling*).
das Feld behaupten ...	to hold the field.
das Feld räumen	to quit the field.
ins Feld rücken	to take the field.
Feld-Apotheker	field apothecary.
Feld-Artillerie	field (and horse) artillery.
Feld-Artillerie-Schiess-Schule	Field Artillery School of Gunnery.
Feldbäckerei	field bakery.
Feldbackofen	field oven.
Feldbahn	field railway (*metre gauge*).
Feldbefestigungskunst ...	art of field fortification.
Feldbinde	waist belt (*officers*).
Feldbrief	letter (*written in the field*).
Felddienst	field service.
Felddienst-Ordnung ...	Field Service Regulations.
Feldeisenbahnwesen ...	field railway service.
Feldflasche	water bottle.
Feldflieger-Abteilung ...	reconnaissance flight.
Feldflugwesen	Field Aviation Service (*obsolete*).
Feldgendarmerie	field police.
Feldgerät	stores.
Feldgeschrei	password.
Feldgeschütz	field gun.

Feldgranate	field gun high explosive (H.E.) shell.
Feld-Haubitze	field howitzer.
Feld-Heer	Field Army.
Feldhose	field service trousers or pantaloons.
Feldjäger	King's Messenger.
Feldjäger (berittener)	mounted courier.
Feldkabelleitung·	cable line.
Feldkanone	field gun.
Feldkessel	mess tin, camp kettle.
Feldkochgerät	field cooking utensils.
Feldkompagnie	field company, *active* *company of a pioneer battalion.*
Feldkoppel	field service belt.
Fold-Krieg	field warfare.
Feld-Kriegs-Kassen-Verwaltung.	field treasury officials.
Feldküche	travelling kitchen.
Feldlazarett	field hospital, casualty clearing station.
Feldluftschiffer-Abteilung (Trupp).	balloon detachment.
Feldmagazin	field depôt.
Feldmarschall	Field-Marshal.
Feld-Maschinen-Gewehr-Zug	machine gun section.
Feldmineurwagen	mining store wagon.
Feldmütze	field service cap.
Feldoberpostinspektion ...	Chief Inspector of Field Post Offices.
Feldoberpostsekretär ...	Chief Field Post Office Secretary.
Feldpatrone	field gun cartridge (*fixed ammunition*).
Feldpionier-Dienst	Text-book of Field Engineering.
Feldpionier-Kompagnie ...	pioneer field company.
Feldpostamt	central field post office.
Feldpostexpedition	branch field post office.
Feldpostmeister	field postmaster.
Feldpoststation	field post office.
Feldrekrutenbataillon ...	recruit battalion in the field.
Feldrekrutendepot	training depôt in the field.
Feldsanitätswesen	Medical Service of the Field Army.
Feldschmiede	field forge.
Feldsignalabteilung	field signalling detachment (*cavalry*).
Feldsignaltrupp	field signal section.
Feldstecher	field glass.
Feldstiefel	field service boots.
Feldtrain-Eskadron ...	field train squadron.
Feldverwaltungs-Behörden ...	field administrative authorities.

Feldverwaltungs-Schreiber ...	superintending clerk.
Feldwache	picket.
Feldwebel	serjeant-major (*company serjeant-major of infantry, pioneers, or foot artillery*).
Feldwebel-Leutnant	serjeant-major-lieutenant (*only appointed in war for depôt or garrison troops*).
Feldwetterstation	meteorological station.
Feldzahlmeister	field paymaster.
Feldzeugmeister	Master of the Ordnance.
Feldzeugmeisterei	Ordnance Department.
Feldzug	campaign.
Feldzugsplan	plan of campaign.
Ferngespräch	telephone conversation.
Fernglas	telescope.
Fernhörer	telephone receiver.
Fernkampfgruppe	long-range group (*artillery*).
Fernpatrouille	distant patrol.
Fernrohr	telescope.
Fernrohraufsatz	telescopic sight.
Fernrohrbüchse	rifle with telescopic sight.
Fernsprecher	telephone.
Fernsprech-Abteilung (Trupp)	telephone detachment (squad).
Fernsprechapparat	telephone instrument.
Fernsprech-Doppelzug ...	Divisional telephone detachment.
Fernsprechgerät	telephone stores.
Fernsprechleitung	telephonic communication, telephone line.
Fernsprechnetz	telephone system.
Fernsprech-Offizier	telephone officer.
Fernsprechstelle	telephone station.
Fernsprechverbindung ... ⎱	telephonic communication.
Fernsprechverkehr ... ... ⎰	
Fernsprechzentral	telephone exchange.
Fernstecher	field glasses.
Fesselballon	captive balloon.
Fester Sitz !	Screw firmly home !
Festlegen (im Plan)	to plot.
Festlegepunkt	reference point.
Festlegung	definition, location, fixing, determination.
Feststellen	to identify, establish, fix.
Feststellung	identification.
Festung	fortress.
Festungen, Kampf um ...	fortress warfare.
Festungsanlagen	fortifications.

Festungsartillerie	fortress artillery.
Festungsbaubeleuchtungstrupp	fortress searchlight section.
Festungsbaufeldwebel ...	fortress construction serjeant-major.
Festungsbauoffiziere	Corps of Fortress Constructors.
Festungsbauwärter	superintendent of fortifications.
Festungsfliegerabteilung ...	fortress flight.
Festungsfunkerabteilung ...	fortress wireless detachment.
Festungsluftschiffertrupp ...	fortress balloon detachment.
Festungsmaschinengewehr-kompagnie.	fortress machine gun company.
Festungsscheinwerferzug ...	fortress searchlight section.
Festungsstab	fortress staff.
Festungswerk	fortification.
Fettdose	box of grease.
Feuer	fire ; bombardment.
Feuer einschalten, eröffnen	to open fire.
Feuer feindwärts verlegen !	Lift your fire !
bei Feuer stehen	to be under fire.
bestreichendes Feuer ...	grazing fire, enfilade fire.
ein heftiges Feuer unterhalten.	to maintain a heavy fire.
lebhaftes Feuer	rapid firing.
ruhiges Feuer	deliberate fire (artillery).
wirksames Feuer	effective fire.
Feuerabriegelung	barrage.
Feuerart	nature of fire (e.g., rapid or deliberate fire).
Feuerbereit	in readiness to open fire.
Feuerbündel	faggots.
Feuererscheinung	flame effect.
Feuergeschwindigkeit ...	rate of fire.
Feuerlärm	fire alarm.
Feuerleitung	fire control, telephone line used for directing fire.
Feuerleitungsübungen ...	fire command exercises.
Feuerleitungsplan	large scale map for fire control.
Feuerlinie	firing line.
Feuerordnung	method of fire (e.g., rapid or deliberate fire).
Feuerpausen	pauses or intervals during firing.
Feuerrichtung	direction of fire.
Feuersäule	column of flame.
Feuerschein	reflection (of gun flash).
Feuerstärke	volume of fire.
Feuerstellung	fire position.
Feuerstellung der Batterie	battery position.
Auswahl der Feuerstellung	selection of battery position,

Feuerstrahl	flash of a gun.
Feuertiefe	depth of fire.
Feuerüberfällen	bursts of fire.
Feuerüberlegenheit	superiority of fire.
Feuervereinigung	concentration of fire.
Feuerverteilung	distribution of fire.
Feuerverteilungsheft	fire distribution book.
Feuerwerker	serjeant-artificer.
Feuerwerks-Offizier	artificer-officer.
Feuerwirkung	fire effect.
Filialdepot	branch depôt.
Filtermasse	drum-contents (*i.e., contents of a gas drum*).
Filzschuh	felt boot.
First	roof of gallery (*mining*).
Flachbahn	flat trajectory.
Flachbahngeschütz	flat trajectory gun.
Flachfeuer	flat trajectory fire.
Flachfeuerbatterie	flat trajectory battery.
Flachswerg	waste, tow waste.
Fladdermine	*sometimes used for* camouflet (*mining*).
Flagge	flag, standard (*naval*).
Flaggenzeichen	flag signals.
Flak (*i.e.*, Flug-Abwehr-Kanone).	anti-aircraft gun.
Flakbatterie	anti-aircraft battery.
Flakgruko (Flug - Abwehr-Kanonen - Gruppen - Kommandeur	A. A. Group Commander.
Flakschutz	anti-aircraft protection.
Flakzug	anti-aircraft section.
Flammenstoss ... ... } Flammenstrahl ... ... }	jet of flame.
Flammenwerfer	"Flammenwerfer" *or* flame projector.
Flammenwerfertrupp	"Flammenwerfer" squad.
Flanke	flank.
Flankenangriff...	flank attack.
Flanken aufdecken	to expose the flanks.
Flankenbewegung	flank march.
Flankenfeuer	enfilade fire, flanking fire.
Flankieren	to enfilade.
Flankierende Stellung ...	position from which enfilade-fire can be brought to bear.
Flankenstollen	branch gallery (*mining*).
Flankierendes Artilleriefeuer ...	enfilade artillery fire.
Flankierung	flanking fire, flanking position.

Flankierungsanlagen	flanking defences.
Flankierungsgeschütze ...	guns for flanking fire.
Flasche	flask, bottle (*has been known to be used for trench mortar bombs*).
Flaschengas	gas from cylinders, cylinder gas.
Flaschensauerstoff	oxygen in cylinders.
Flaschenzug	pulley.
Flechtwerk	hurdle-work.
Flickmaterial	material for repair of clothing.
Fliegende Brücke	flying bridge.
Fliegende Division	independent Division.
Fliegende Kolonne	flying column.
Flieger	aviator ; airman.
Fliegerabteilung	flight.
Fliegerabwehr	anti-aircraft measures.
Fliegeraufnahme	aeroplane photograph.
Fliegerbeobachtung	aeroplane observation.
Fliegerbeschuss	anti-aircraft firing.
Fliegerdeckung !	" Put on the screens ! " ; keeping under cover from aeroplanes.
Fliegerdeckung aufgehoben !	" Remove screens."
Fliegerkampf	aerial combat.
Fliegerkompagnie	flying company (Bavaria) (*now obsolete*)
Fliegerkorn	foresight (*on rifle : for use against aerial objectives*).
Fliegerphotographien ...	aeroplane photographs.
Fliegerschiessen	anti-aircraft fire.
Fliegersicht	view from aircraft.
Fliegertauglichkeit	fitness for flying.
Fliegertruppen...	Flying Troops (*equivalent to aeroplane units of Royal Flying Corps*).
Fliegertuch	linen sheet (*for signalling to aeroplanes*).
Fliegerwarnungsdienst ...	arrangements for giving warning of the approach of aircraft.
Fliehbolzen	centrifugal bolt (*in fuze, &c.*).
Floss	(*a*) float, raft ; (*b*) fin, steadying fin in a dirigible.
Flossbrücke	floating bridge.
Flottenatmer	a *rescue apparatus similar to the* " Dräger Selbstretter " *or oxygen breathing apparatus.*
Flüchtige Befestigung ...	hasty entrenchment.
Flug	flight.
Flug-Abwehr-Kanone (Flak)	anti-aircraft gun.
Flug-Abwehr-Kanonen-Zug ...	anti-aircraft section.
Flugbahn	trajectory.

Flügel	...	wing, flank ; aileron.
Flügel-Adjutant	... ...	Aide-de-camp to the Emperor.
Flügelfeder ...	... ...	wing tip.
Flügelkompagnie	... ...	wing company.
Flügelmutter ...	... ...	wing nuts.
Flügelweise ...	... ...	side by side.
Flügelzug ...	... ...	flank platoon.
linker Flügelzug	... ...	platoon on left wing of sector.
Flugzeuggeschwader ...	...	squadron of aeroplanes.
Flugmaschine ...	... ...	aeroplane.
Flugplatz ...	... ...	aerodrome.
Flugwesen ...	... ...	aviation.
Flugzeug	...	aeroplane.
Ft.-Flugzeug ...	...	aeroplane fitted with wireless.
Flugzeugführer ...	...	pilot (of aeroplane).
Flugzeugsschuppen ...	...	aeroplane shed, hangar.
Förderbahn	...	field tramway (60 cm. gauge).
Formation	...	formation.
Fortifikations-Beamte	...	engineer official.
Fortlaufende Eindeckungen		continuous recesses (under parapet).
Franzosenwache ...	...	guard for French prisoners of war.
Freiliegen ...	...	to be unencumbered.
Freimachen (des Schussfeldes)		clearing (the field of fire).
Freisprechen	...	to acquit.
Freiwillige Krankenpflege	...	voluntary aid.
Freiwilliger	...	volunteer.
Freiwilliges Automobilkorps...		Volunteer Automobile Corps.
Freiwilliges Motorboot-Korps		Volunteer Motorboat Corps.
Fressbeutel	...	nose bag.
Frieden...	...	peace.
ein fauler Frieden ...	...	a hollow truce.
Friedensmässig ...	...	obtaining in peace time.
Friedensfahrplan ...	...	peace time table (railway).
Friedensfuss	...	peace footing.
Friedenspräsenzstärke	...	peace strength law.
Friedensstand ...	...	peace conditions.
Frontausdehnung ...	...	extent of front held.
Frontbeobachtungsstelle	...	forward observing station.
Frontlänge	...	frontage, front.
Front machen ...	...	to front.
Front-Offizier ...	...	regimental officer.
Frontstärke	...	the fighting troops.
Frühsprenger	...	premature burst.
Fühlung	...	touch.
in engster Fühlung bleiben		to remain in closest touch.
Führen	...	to lead, guide, convey.
Führer	...	commander, leader, guide.

Führer der gr. Bagage ...	commander of the train.
Fuhre	transport.
eine Fuhre Heu	a load of hay.
Fuhrkost	travelling expenses.
Fuhrpark	transport park.
Fuhrparkkolonne	supply park.
Fuhrparkwagen	supply park vehicle.
Führung	Higher Command ; conduct ; guiding.
Führungsring	driving band (*of a projectile*).
Fufa (Funker-Feld-Abteilung)	field wireless detachment.
Fukla (Funker-Klein-Abteilung)	trench wireless detachment.
Füllpulver 02 (Fp. 02) ...	1902 pattern explosive (T.N.T.).
Füllstoff	liquid (*used to fill gas shell*).
Füllung	the bursting charge of a shell.
Funken...	to spark ; to send a wireless message, transmit by wireless.
Funkenapparat	wireless apparatus.
Funken-Empfangstation ...	wireless receiving station.
Funkenstation...	wireless station.
Leichte Funkenstation ...	light wireless station.
Schwere Funkenstation ...	heavy wireless station.
Funken-Telegraphen-Abteilung	wireless telegraph detachment.
Funkentelegraphie (Ft.) ...	wireless telegraphy (W/T.)
Ft. Dienst	wireless telegraphy.
Ft. Einrichtung	wireless installation.
Ft.-Flugzeug	aeroplane fitted with wireless.
Versagen der F.T.	breakdown of wireless apparatus.
Funker	wireless operator.
Funkerabteilung	wireless detachment.
Funkerfeldabteilung	field wireless detachment.
Funkerkleinabteilung... ...	trench wireless detachment.
Funkerkommando	wireless headquarters.
Funkerkompagnie	wireless telegraph company (*peace*)
Funkspruch	wireless message.
Funktionieren	to work (*mechanical term*).
Furagierleine	forage cord.
Furier	quartermaster-serjeant (*for supply*)
Füsilier...	private of fusilier battalion *or* regiment.
Fuss-Artillerie	foot artillery.
Fuss-Artillerie-Schiess-Schule	Foot Artillery School of Gunnery.
Fusslappen	foot bandages.
Fussscheiben	discs for feet of trestles (*bridging*).
Futter	fodder, forage ; lining of clothes.
Futtersack	corn sack.
Futterwagen	forage wagon.

G.

Gabel	fork; bracket (*in ranging*).
Gabeln (einen Schacht) ...	to run out a branch gallery (*mining*).
Gabeln, sich	to branch off (*mining*).
Galerie	cross gallery (*mining*).
Gamaschen	gaiters, leggings.
Gang	gait, pace, step; carriage, bearing; alley (*trench*); course or progress (*of events, fight, &c.*).
ausser Gang sein	to be out of gear (*machinery*).
Ganzboot	cavalry pontoon composed of two half-pontoons ("*Halbbooten*").
Ganzponton	whole pontoon of the Corps equipment (*as opposed to "Halbponton," bipartite pontoon*).
Garbe (eines Maschinen-Gewehrs).	cone of bullets of a machine gun.
Garde	Guard.
Garde-Regiment zu Fuss (G.R. z.F.).	Foot Guards Regiment.
Gardes du Corps	(*not translated; the "Gardes du Corps" Regiment is one of the Guard Cavalry Regiments.*)
Gardist	private of Foot Guards and Body Guard regiments (*e.g.*, 115th).
Garnison-Bauwesen	Barrack Construction Department.
Garnisondienst	garrison duty.
Garnisondienstfähig	fit for garrison duty.
Garnisondiensttauglich ...	
Garnisonsauditeur	Garrison Judge-Advocate.
Garnisonsbataillon	garrison battalion.
Garnisonslazarett	garrison hospital.
Garnisonsverwendungsfähig ...	fit for garrison duty.
Garnison-Verwaltung... ...	garrison administrative officials.
Garnison-Verwaltungs-Direktor	Director of Garrison Administration.
Garnison-Verwaltungs-Inspektor.	Inspector of Garrison Administration.
Garnison - Verwaltungs - Ober-Inspektor.	Chief Inspector of Garrison Administration.
Gasalarm	gas alarm.
Gasabwehrmittel	means of defence against gas.
Gasangriff	gas attack.
Gasbereitschaft	gas readiness, precautions against gas, "gas alert."

Gasbereitschaft (erhöhte) ...	" special gas alert."
Gasflasche	gas cylinder.
Gasgranate	gas shell.
Gaskampf	gas warfare.
Gaskolonne	gas column (*balloon troops*).
Gaskrank	" gassed."
Gasmaskpatrone	gas mask drum.
Gasmine	*Minenwerfer* gas shell.
Halbe schwere Gasmine ...	half-sized heavy *Minenwerfer* gas shell.
Mittlere Gasmine	medium *Minenwerfer* gas shell.
Leichte Gasmine	light *Minenwerfer* gas shell.
Gaspipette	gas sampling tube.
Gasschutzpäckchen	anti-gas respirator.
Gasschutzbrillen	gas goggles.
Gasschutzmaske	gas mask, helmet.
Gasschutz-Offizier (G.S.O.) ...	anti-gas officer.
Gassumpf	gas pocket.
Gasvergiftet	" gassed."
Gaswolke	gas cloud.
Gattung	arm of the service.
Gaze	gauze.
Gebiet	area, district.
Gebirgshaubitze	mountain howitzer.
Gebirgskanone	mountain gun.
Gebirgskrieg	mountain warfare.
Gebirgs - Maschinen - Gewehr - Abteilung	mountain machine gun detachment.
Gebirgs - Minenwerfer Kompagnie	mountain *Minenwerfer* company.
Gebiss	set of teeth ; bit for horses.
Stangengebiss	curb.
Trensengebiss	snaffle.
Geerdet werden	to be earthed (*electrical*).
Gefahr	danger, risk, peril.
Gefährden	to endanger, risk, imperil.
Gefahrlosigkeit	safety.
Gefahrsmomenten	critical moments.
Gefangenenaussage	prisoners' statements.
einen Gefangenen verhören	to interrogate a prisoner.
Gefangenentransport ...	convoy of prisoners.
Gefangener	prisoner.
Gefecht...	fight, fighting, engagement, action, combat, battle.
ausser Gefecht gezetzt werden	to be put out of action.
ein hinhaltendes Gefecht ...	a containing action.

Gefechtsabschnitt	battle sector.
Gefechtsauftrag	objective.
Gefechtsbagage	first line transport.
Gefechtsbataillon	battalion in line.
Gefechtsbatterie	firing battery.
Gefechtsbefehl...	operation order.
Gefechtsbefehlstellung ...	battle headquarters.
Gefechtsbereitschaft	readiness for action.
Gefechtsbereitschaft (erhöhte)	increased readiness for action ; " stand to."
Gefechtsbereitschaft (höchste)	instant readiness for action ; " stand to."
Gefechtsbericht	tactical report.
Gefechtsbreiten	frontages.
Gefechtsfall	engagement.
Gefechtsfeld	battlefield, scene of action.
Gefechts-Ft-Station	wireless station near the firing line.
Gefechtshandlung	conduct of operations.
Gefechtslage	tactical situation *or* conditions.
Gefechtsordonnanz	orderly, runner.
Gefechtsstaffel...	wagon line (*of a field battery in action*).
Gefechtsstand	battle headquarters.
Gefechtsstärke	fighting strength.
Gefechtsstelle	battle headquarters, command post.
Gefechtsstellung	battle station.
Gefechtsstreifen	battle zone, zone of combat.
Gefechtstätigkeit	action during an operation.
Gefechtszweck...	objective, tactical consideration.
Geflecht	plaiting, hurdle-work, wicker-work.
Gefreitenknopf	*button (small) worn on collar as badge of rank for lance-corporal.*
Gefreiter	lance-corporal, acting bombardier.
Gegenangriff	counter-attack.
Gegenbefehl	counter-order.
Gegenmassregeln	counter-measures.
Gegenmine	countermine (*mining*).
Gegenstand	article, object, affair.
Gegenstoss	counter-thrust, counter-attack.
Gegner	enemy, opponent, foe.
Gegnerisch	hostile.
Gehalt	pay (*of officers*).
Geheim (geh :)...	secret.
streng geheim	strictly secret.
Geheimschrift	cipher, code.
Gehöft	farm.
Gehölz	copse.

Gehorsamsverweigerung ...	refusal to obey orders.
Geisel	hostage.
Geistlicher	chaplain.
Geladen (gel.)	loaded.
Gelände	ground, country, terrain.
abfallendes Gelände ...	a falling slope.
aufsteigendes Gelände ...	a rising slope.
bedecktes Gelände	close country.
durchschnittenes Gelände ...	intersected country, close country.
freies Gelände	open country.
welliges Gelände	undulating country.
Geländeabschnitt	area.
Geländefalte	fold in the ground.
Geländegestalt	nature of the ground.
Geländekunde	topography.
Geländepunkt	topographical feature.
Geländerhölzer	uprights for handrails (bridging).
Geländerleine	railrope (bridging).
Geländespiegel	panoramic mirror, periscope.
Geländeteil	area.
Geländeverhältnisse	nature of the ground.
Geländewinkel...	angle of sight.
Gelegenheitsziel	fleeting target.
Geleise (Gleis)	line of rails or track (railway).
Geleit ... ... ⎫ Geleitmannschaft ... ... ⎭	escort.
Gelenkstab	jointed stick.
Gelingen	to succeed, be successful.
Gemeinde	commune.
Gemeiner	private soldier.
Gendarme	gendarme.
Gendarmerie	military police.
Gendarmerie-Wachtmeister ...	serjeant-major of the gendarmerie.
Genehmigt	approved.
General...	General.
General-Adjutant	Aide-de-Camp to the Emperor.
Generalarzt	Colonel (medical).
General-Auditeur	Judge-Advocate-General.
Generaldelegierte	Delegate-General (at Army H.Q. in connection with " voluntary aid ").
General der Artillerie... ...	General of Artillery (commands a Corps).
General der Infanterie ...	General of Infantry (commands a Corps).
General der Kavallerie ...	General of Cavalry (commands a Corps).
General-Feldmarschall ...	Field-Marshal (usually commands a Group of Armies).

General-Inspekteur des Etappen- und Eisenbahnwesens.	Inspector-General of Lines of Communication and Railways.
General-Intendant	Intendant-General.
Generalität	General Officers.
General-Kommando	Staff of an Army Corps, Corps Headquarters.
Generalleutnant	Lieutenant-General (*commands a Division*).
Generalmajor	Major-General (*commands a Brigade*).
General-Oberst	" General-Oberst " (*usually commands an Army*).
Generaloberarzt	Lieutenant-Colonel (*medical*).
Generalprofoss	Provost-Marshal.
General-Quartiermeister ...	Quartermaster-General at G.H.Q. (*a General Staff officer*).
Generalstab	General Staff.
Generalstabsarzt	Lieutenant-General (Director-General of Medical Services).
Obergeneralarzt und Sanitäts-Inspekteur.	Major-General (*medical*).
Generalarzt	Colonel (*medical*).
Generaloberarzt	Lieutenant-Colonel (*medical*).
Oberstabsarzt	Major (*medical*).
Stabsarzt	Captain (*medical*).
Assistenzarzt	Second-Lieutenant (*medical*).
Generalstäbler...	General Staff Officer (*unofficially used instead of " Generalstabs-Offizier "*).
Generalstabschef	Chief of the General Staff.
Generalstabskarte	staff map.
Generalstabs-Offizier	General Staff officer.
Generalveterinär	Colonel (*veterinary*).
Genesungsabteilung	convalescent depôt.
Genesungskompagnie	convalescent company.
Genesendekompagnie	
Genesungsheim	sanatorium, convalescent home.
Genfer Abkommen	Geneva Convention.
Geniekorps	Corps of Engineers.
Geniewesen	engineering.
Gent Minenwerfer	(*not translated*).
Geöffnet	at full interval.
Geöffneter Linie (Batterie in)	battery in line at full interval.
Gepäck ... ·	pack, kit, baggage.
Gepäck ablegen	to take off packs.
Gepäckbretter	kit-boards (*railway transport*).
Gepäcklatten	kit-stanchions (*railway transport*).
Geplänkel	skirmish among outposts.

Gerade	straight ; even.
gerade Rotten	even files.
ungerade Rotten	odd files.
Gerät (e)	stores ; implements.
Artilleriegeräte	artillery equipment.
Gerät fordern	to indent for stores.
Gerätedepot	store depôt.
Gerätewagen	pioneer store wagon.
Gerichtsdienst	court martial duty.
Gerippe	framework.
Geröllboden	rubble, loose ground (e.g., at the bottom of a mine crater).
Gesamtstärke	total strength.
Geschäftszimmer	orderly room, office.
Geschickt	skilful, clever, wise.
Geschirr	harness ; gear, utensils (e.g., cooking).
Geschirrtau	trace-rope.
Geschlossen	closed, in close order, at close interval.
geschlossene Schützengräben	closed works.
Geschoss	projectile, bullet, shell.
Brand-Geschoss	incendiary shell.
Geschosse (zu kurz gehende)	" shorts."
Granate-Geschoss	H.E. shell.
Geschossart	nature, type, kind or pattern of projectile.
Geschossaufschlag	fall of the shell.
Geschossbahn	trajectory.
Geschossgarbe	cone of fire (of bullets, &c.).
Geschosskopf	head (of shell).
Geschosssicher	shell-proof (not bomb-proof) ; (also " bullet-proof," but this depends on context).
Geschosstrichter	shell crater, shell hole.
Geschütz	gun.
Geschützbedienung	gun crew.
Geschützbettung	gun platform.
Geschützeinschnitt	gun pit.
Geschützführer	gun captain.
Geschützkampf	artillery duel.
Geschützpark	gun park.
Geschützrohr	barrel of a gun.
Geschützstand...	gun emplacement.
Geschützzwischenraum ...	interval between guns.
Geschwader	squadron (naval or air service).
Geschwindigkeit	speed, rapidity, velocity ; rate of fire.

Geschwindschritt (im)	...	at the double.
Gesicht	...	face ; sight, vision.
Gesichtsfeld ⎫ Gesichtskreis ⎬ ...	...	field of vision *or* view.
Gesichtspunkt ...	...	aspect, point of view.
Gesuch	...	request.
Getreidefeld	...	cornfield.
Getrennt	...	separated, isolated.
Getriebe	...	driving-gear.
Getriebholz	...	frames and sheeting (*as opposed to* " *Schurzholz*," *or continuous casing in mining*).
Gewähr...	...	guarantee.
Gewährleisten ...	...	ensure, guarantee, enable.
Gewalt	...	power, force.
Gewaltmarsch ...	...	forced march.
Gewaltsam	...	vigorous, powerful, heavy (*attack*).
Gewandt	...	intelligent, smart, skilful.
Gewehr	...	rifle.
An die Gewehre ! ...	...	Stand to !
Gewehr ab ! ...	...	Order arms !
Gewehr auf ! ...	...	Shoulder arms !
Gewehr über ! ...	...	Slope arms !
mit Gewehr bei Fuss stehen		to be at the order.
Gewehrbatterie ...	...	rifle battery.
Gewehrfeuer	...	rifle fire.
Gewehrführer ...	...	gun captain (*machine gun*).
Gewehrgestell ...	...	rifle rack.
Gewehrgranate (14) ...	...	(1914 pattern) rifle grenade.
Gewehrgranatengestell	...	rifle grenade stand.
Gewehrhaken	...	rifle clips.
Gewehrkolben ...	...	butt of rifle.
Gewehrpanzergeschoss	...	armour-piercing bullet.
Gewehrpyramide ...	...	piled arms.
Gewehrriemen ...	...	rifle sling.
Gewehrschaft	...	stock of rifle.
Gewehrschloss ...	...	breech mechanism of rifle.
Gewehrstutz -(stütze)	...	arm rack.
Gewehrträger	...	apparatus for carrying a machine gun.
Gewehrtragende ...	...	men who carry rifles.
Gewehrweise	...	in order of guns.
Gezeichnet (gez.) ...	...	signed (*in copies of documents*).
Gezogen	...	rifled.
Gitterbrücke	...	lattice girder bridge.
Gkofunk	...	Corps Wireless H.Q.
Glatt	...	smooth, smooth bore.
Gleichschritt	...	march in step.

Gleichstrom	continuous current (*electrical*).
Gleis (Geleise)	line of rails *or* track (*railway*).
Gleisbreite	wheel track.
Gleitbahn	slipway.
Gleitflug	volplane.
Glied	rank.
Gliedern	to organize.
Gliedern nach der Tiefe ...	to organize in depth.
Gliederung	distribution, organization.
Kriegsgliederung	order of battle.
Glockenzeichen	signals given by gongs.
Glühzündapparat	dynamo-exploder.
Glühzünder	electric fuze.
Graben	trench.
erster Graben	front trench.
zweiter Graben	support trench.
dritter Graben	reserve trench.
Annäherungsgraben ...	communication *or* approach trench.
Laufgraben	communication trench.
Verbindungsgraben ...	
Verkehrsgraben	supervision *or* lateral communication trench.
Grabenbekleidung	revetment.
Grabenbesatzung	men in the trenches, trench garrison.
Grabenposten	sentries in the fire trenches.
Grabenrost	duck boards.
Grabensohle	sole *or* bottom of trench.
Grabenspiegel	trench mirror.
Grabenstärke	trench strength.
Grabenstück	length *or* section of trench.
Grabentiefe	depth of trench.
Grabenwand	side of trench.
Grad	degree.
Gradabzeichen	badge of rank.
Gradbogen	graduated arc ; sextant.
Granate	high explosive (H.E.) shell.
Granate (Spreng-)	
Granate-Geschoss	
Granateinschlag	shell burst.
Granatenhülse	shell case.
Granatenwerfer	" stick " bomb-thrower (*usually not translated*).
Granatfüllung	bursting charge of shell.
Granatloch	shell hole.
Granatring	driving band on shell.
Granattrichter...	shell crater, shell hole.

Granatwerfer	*see* " Granatenwerfer " (*for which it is a recent contraction*).
Granatwurfmine Lanz (Gr. W.M.L.)	9·1-cm. Lanz *Minenwerfer* H.E. shell.
Granat-Zünder (Gr. Z.) ...	percussion fuze for H.E. shell.
Grasschollen	sods.
Grate	scorings (*e.g.*, *in the bore of a gun*).
Grauguss	cast iron.
Greifzangen	grip straps (*bridging*).
Grenadier	grenadier.
Grenadier-Regiment	grenadier regiment.
Grenze	limit, boundary, frontier.
Grenzegruppen	flank groups (*of a unit in the trenches*).
Grenzewächter ⎱ Grenzwache ⎰	frontier guard.
Griffhebel	lever (*of breech mechanism*).
Groftrupp (Grosser-Flammenwerfer-Trupp).	large *Flammenwerfer* squad.
Gros	main body.
Grosse Bagage	baggage section of the train.
Grosser Generalstab	Great General Staff.
Grosses Hauptquartier ...	General Headquarters.
Grundlinie	base line, datum line.
Grundriss	design, sketch, plan.
Grundsatz	principle.
Grundsohle	mine level.
Grundwasser	surface water.
Grundzahlen	theoretical figures, not allowing for error (*artillery*).
Grünkreuzmunition	" green cross " gas shell.
Gruppe	Group (*equivalent to a Corps*) or group (8 *men under a N.C.O.*).
Gruppenfeuer	volley firing.
Gruppenführer	group commander.
Gulaschkanone	travelling kitchen (*colloquial*).
Gummi	rubber, india-rubber.
Gurt	girth, belt (*machine gun*).
Tragegurt	belt (*e.g.*, *for carrying an infantry shield, &c.*).
Gürtel	belt.
S.M. in Gürteln	S.A.A. in belts.
Gürtelbahn	circular railway.
Gürten	to fill a machine gun belt.
Gurtstelle	belt store (*machine gun*).
Guttaperchazündschnur ...	gutta-percha safety fuze.

H.

Haarbusch	plume.
Hacke	pick.
Häcksel	chaff.
Hafendirektion	Harbour Directorate.
Haft	arrest, imprisonment ; clasp, holder.
Haftpfahl	hook-picket.
Haftpflock	steel picket (*bridging*).
Hahn	cock, tap.
den Hahn am Gewehr spannen	to cock a rifle.
Hahnspitz	striker (*of a pistol*).
Haken und Ösen	hooks and eyes.
Halbmesser	diameter.
Halbponton	half-pontoon (*of the bipartite Divisional equipment*).
Halfter	halter, headcollar ; holster.
Halfterriemen	head rope.
Halsbinde	scarf.
Halt ! Wer da ?	Halt ! Who goes there ?
Halter, falzartiger	grooved charger or strip (*magazine rifle*).
Haltung	carriage, bearing, behaviour.
Handbetriebbahn	trench tramway (50 *cm. gauge*).
Handfeuerwaffen	small arms.
Handgemenge	hand to hand fight.
Handgranate	hand grenade.
Behelfshandgranate	extemporised hand grenade.
Brandhandgranate	incendiary hand grenade.
entschärfte Handgranate	hand grenade without detonator.
scharfe Handgranate	live hand grenade.
scharf machen	to insert a detonator in.
Stielhandgranate	cylindrical grenade with handle.
Übungshandgranate	dummy hand grenade.
Handgranatenkapsel	detonator for hand grenade.
Handgranatennische	grenade recess.
Handgranatenoffizier	bombing officer.
Handgranatenstand	ground set aside for hand grenade training.
Handgranatentrupp	bombing party.
Handgranatenwerfer	"thrower," bomber.
Handgriff	handle.
Handhabung	handling, use, drill.
Handlüfter	rotary blower (*mining*).

Handpferd	led horse.
Handschuh	glove.
Handschutz	hand guard (*rifle*).
Handseite	off side (" *Sattelseite*," *near side*).
Handwaffen	small arms.
Handwerker	workman, tradesman, artisan, artificer.
Handwerkerabteilung ...	artificer's detachment.
Handwerkerabteilung des Trains.	tradesmen of the Train.
Handwerksmeister	master mechanic.
Handwerkszeug	tools.
Handwerkskiste	tool box.
Hang	slope; deep level (*in mining*).
Hängematte	hammock.
Hartfutter	corn (*ration*).
Hartschier (Hatschier) ...	halbardier, archer, soldier of the Bavarian Body Guard of Halbardiers.
Hartspiritus	solidified alcohol, solidified methylated spirits.
Haubitze	howitzer.
Küsten-Haubitze	coast defence howitzer.
Turm-Haubitze	howitzer in turret.
Leichte (Schwere) Feld-Haubitze.	light (heavy) field howitzer.
Haubitz-Batterie	howitzer battery.
Haubitz-Granate	howitzer shell.
Haubitz-Zünder	howitzer fuze.
Haufen	dump (*mining*).
Hauptarm	main gallery (*mining*).
Hauptgestell	head stall.
Hauptinhalt	synopsis.
Hauptkadettenanstalt ...	Central Cadet Institution (Gross Lichterfelde).
Hauptkampflinie	main fighting line.
Hauptkrankenbuch ...	hospital register.
Hauptleute und Rittmeister...	Captains (*of dismounted and mounted arms*).
Hauptlinie	axis.
Hauptmacht	main body.
Hauptmann	Captain (*of infantry, artillery or engineers*).
Hauptmesstelle...	principal survey station.
Hauptquartier...	headquarters.
Grosses Hauptquartier ...	General Headquarters.
Hauptstellung	main position, main emplacement.

Hauptstollen	main gallery (*mining*).
Haupttrupp	main body of advanced guard.
Hauptverbandplatz	main dressing station, casualty clearing station.
Hebebaum	lever, handspike.
Heer	Army.
das stehende Heer	Standing Army.
Heeresgruppe	Group of Armies.
Heeres-Kavallerie	Independent Cavalry.
Heeresleitung, Oberste ...	Commander-in-Chief, General Headquarters, Higher Command.
Heereszeitung	Army Gazette.
Heimat	home (*usually translated as Germany, &c.*).
Heimatsgebiet...	The Home Territory.
Heimatsheer	The Home Army (*as opposed to "Feldheer"*).
Helm	helmet.
Helmüberzug	helmet cover.
Hemmkette	drag-chain.
Hemmklotz	brake-shoe ; block placed behind a wheel to prevent a cart moving backwards down a slope.
Hemmschuh	drag-shoe.
Hemmung	jam (*machine gun*).
Henkel	handle (*of a camp kettle*).
Heran	up.
Heranführung	supply.
Heranmarschieren	to march up, come up, approach.
Heranschaffen	to bring up (*e.g., ammunition*).
Heranschleichen	to creep forward (up).
Heranziehen	to detail ; to bring up.
Heranziehung	requisitioning (*e.g., of horses*).
Herausziehen	to withdraw.
Herbstmanöver	autumn manœuvres.
Hereinmarsch	march into the trenches.
Hergestellte	recovered wounded.
Herrschen	to rule, reign, prevail.
Herstellung	fitting, fixing up, construction. production,
Hervorlocken	to entice out, to draw (*e.g., fire*).
Hilfeleistung	rescue work, first aid.
Hilfsbahn	auxiliary railway.
Hilfsbeobachter	auxiliary observer.
Hilfsdienstpflicht	auxiliary service act.
Hilfskorn	auxiliary foresight (*rifle*).
Hilfskräfte	auxiliary personnel.

Hilfslazarett	auxiliary hospital.
Hilfslazarettzug	auxiliary ambulance train.
Hilfstruppen	auxiliary troops.
Hilfsziel	aiming point.
Himmel, am	" in the air."
Hindernis	obstacle, wire entanglement, " wire."
elektrische Hindernisse ...	electrified wire entanglements.
versenktes Hindernis ...	sunken obstacle.
Hinten (nach)	in rear.
Hinterhalt	ambush.
Hintergelände...	ground behind the line, back area.
Hintergestell eines Wagens ...	back part of a wagon.
Hinterkaffe	stern (of a pontoon).
Hinterlader	breech-loader.
Hinterwagen	wagon body.
Hin- und Rückleitung ...	complete metallic circuit.
Hinweis	indication, direction, reference.
Hirschfänger	short hunting knife.
Hoboist	bandsman.
Hochbahn	elevated railway.
Hochdruck	high pressure (mining).
Hochempfindlich	highly sensitive (of a telephone, &c.).
Hochspannungsleitung ...	high tension wire.
Hochstand	raised, commanding or elevated position.
Höchstzahl	maximum.
Hocken...	to crouch.
hockende Schützen im Graben.	troops sitting in trenches.
Höhenrauch	haze.
Höhenrichtmaschine	elevating gear.
Höhenrücken	ridge, crest.
Hohltraverse	hollow traverse.
Hohlweg	sunken road.
Holz	wood.
Holzattrappe	wooden dummy (e.g., bomb for instructional purposes).
Holzbauten	wooden buildings.
Holzdeckel	wooden lid or plug.
Holzfäller-Abteilung	tree-felling detachment.
Holzhammer	mallet.
Holzkästen zum Sümpfen ...	wooden sump boxes.
Holzkohle	charcoal.
Holzmeissel	wood chisel.
Holzrahmen	wooden frame.
Holzscheibe	wooden target.

Holzwolle	...	wood shavings.
Horchapparat ...	...	listening apparatus (*mining*).
Horchdienst	...	listening methods.
Horchen	...	to listen.
es wird gehorcht ...	...	a " listen " will be made.
Horchergebnis ...	...	results of listening.
Horchgang	...	listening gallery.
Horchmeldung ...	...	listening report.
Horchminengang ...	...	listening gallery.
Horchpatrouille ...	...	listening patrol.
Horchpause	...	listening period (*mining, &c.*).
Horchposten	...	listening post, listening sentry.
Horchpostengraben ...	...	listening post sap.
Horchpostenloch ...	...	listening post.
Horchsappe	...	listening sap.
Horchstollen	...	listening gallery.
Horchzeit	...	listening time.
Hornist...	...	bugler.
Horn	...	bugle, horn (*musical instrument and horn of cattle, &c.*).
Huf	...	hoof.
Hufeisen ...	...	horse-shoe.
Hufeisentasche	...	shoe-case.
Hufkratzer	...	hoof-pick.
Hülle	...	cover (*e.g., for breech of rifle*).
Ladungshülle ...	...	} canister bomb.
Minenhülle	...	
Hüllen	...	casing (*mining*).
Hülse (Patronen-)	...	cartridge case.
Hundetrupp ...	...	dog detachment.
Hupen	...	to hoot (*aeroplane doing contact work*).
Hupsignal	...	hooting signal (*aeroplane*).
Husar	...	hussar.
Husaren-Regiment ...	...	hussar regiment.

I.

Impfen	to vaccinate, inoculate.
Impfliste	vaccination list.
Infanterie	infantry.
Infanterieausbildung	infantry training.
Infanterie-Flieger	infantry aeroplane, contact patrol.
Infanteriegeschütz	" infantry gun."
Infanteriegeschützbatterie	battery of " infantry guns."
Infanterie-Konstruktions-Bureau	Infantry Technical Section (of Technical Institute).
Infanterie-Munitions-Kolonne	infantry ammunition column (heavy).
Infanteriepionierkompagnie	infantry pioneer company.
Infanteriereglement	" Infantry Training " (*abbreviation of " Exerzier-Reglement für die Infanterie* ").
Infanterie-Schiess-Schule	School of Musketry.
Infanterie-Sturm-Batterie	infantry assault battery.
Infanterist	infantry soldier.
Ingenieur-Komitee	Engineer Committee.
Ingenieur-Korps	the Corps of Engineers (*as distinct from the Corps of Pioneers*).
Inhaltsangabe	statement of contents.
Inhaltsverzeichnis	list of contents.
Innenwache	inlying picket.
Innen-Zünder	internal fuze.
Inselwache-Bataillon	coast defence battalion.
Inspekteur	Inspector-General.
Inspektion	Inspection (*or district, &c., under an inspector*).
Instandhaltung	maintenance.
Instandsetzung	repair.
Instellunggehen (das)	going into the line.
Intendant	" Intendant " (*not translated ; an Intendant is an administrative official*).
Intendantur	Intendance (*i.e., the service dealing with pay, finance, barracks, supply, and clothing*).
Intendantur-Assessor	Intendance assessor.
Intendantur-Beamte	Intendance officials.
Intendantur-Rat	Intendance councillor.
Intendantur-Registrator	Intendance registrar.
Intendantur-Sekretär	Intendance clerk.
Interimsbahn	temporary railway.
Intervalle (Zwischenraum)	interval.

Irrung ...	...	...	...	error.
Isolator...	...	...	...	insulator (*electrical*).
Isolierband	...	...	...	insulating tape.
Isoliert ...	...	...	...	isolated; insulated.
Iststand ⎫ Iststärke ⎬	...	...	...	⎧ actual strength (*as opposed to* ⎨ "*Etatsstärke*" or *establishment*).
I-Träger	...	...	...	steel joists and girders.

J.

Jacke	jacket.
Jagdstaffel	pursuit flight (*aviation unit*).
Jäger	" Jäger " (*not translated ; corresponds to our "Rifles" or "rifleman"*).
Jäger zu Pferde	" Jäger zu Pferde " (*not translated ; the title of certain cavalry regiments*).
Jahresklasse	yearly class of recruits, annual recruit contingent.
Jahrgang	
Joch	bay (*of bridge*).
Jochbrücke	pile bridge.
Jod	iodine.
Jodtinktur	tincture of iodine.
Jugend-Kompagnie	a military training company for boys.
Jugend-Wehr	organization for giving boys a semi-military training.

K.

K-Munition	armour-piercing ammunition (*rifle or machine gun*).
Kabel ... ... Kabeldraht	} cable.
Kabelleitung	cable line.
Kabelstrecke	length of cable.
Kabelkiste	test box.
Kadettenhaus ... ... Kadettenschule	} cadet school.
Kagol (Kampfflugzeug-Geschwader, Oberste Heeresleitung).	Battle-plane Squadron under G.H.Q.
Kahnfähre	ferry by rowing boat.
Kaiserliche Kommissar u. Militär-Inspekteur.	Imperial Commissioner (*of voluntary aid units*).
Kaliber...	calibre (*gun, rifle &c.*).
schweres Kaliber (15 u. 21 cm.)	heavy artillery (15 and 21 cm.).
kleinkalibrig	small bore.
Kalipatrone	potash-cartridge.
Kammer	chamber, bolt (*of rifle*).
Kammerhülse	central tube (*of shrapnel*).
Kammerknopf...	knob (*of rifle bolt*).
Kammerunteroffizier	N.C.O. or quartermaster in charge of clothing.
Kampf	battle, fight, combat, engagement, action.
Kampferfahrung	experience of fighting.
Kampfflugzeug-Geschwader ...	battle-plane squadron (= 6 *battle-plane flights*).
Kampffront	front line, fighting front.
Kampfgas	battle gas.
Kampfhandlung	method of fighting.
Kampflage	tactical situation.
Kampfmittel	means of warfare.
Kampfstaffel	battle-plane flight (= 6 *battle-planes*).
Kampftagesrate	daily allotment of gun ammunition for active operations.
Kampfunfähig zu machen ...	to put out of action.
Kampfverhältnisse	tactical situation.
Kampfzweck	objective.
Kaninchenlöcher	" funk holes " (*recesses under parapet*).

C

Kanne	can (*of a food carrier*).
Kanone	gun.
Küstenkanone	coast defence gun.
Mantelkanone	jacketed gun.
Marinekanone	naval gun.
Revolverkanone	revolver gun.
Ringkanone	gun with chase rings.
Turmkanone	gun in turret.
Schützengrabenkanone ...	trench gun.
Kanonen-Granate	gun shell.
Kanonen-Zünder	gun fuze.
Kanonier	gunner.
Kantine	canteen.
Kappe	cap (*e.g., of fuze, shell, &c.*).
Kapelle...	band.
Kapellmeister	bandmaster.
Kapitulant	re-engaged man.
Kapitulieren (um weiter zu dienen).	to re-engage.
Kapitulieren (einer Festung)	to surrender, capitulate.
Kapsel	detonator.
Kapuze...	cape.
Karabiner	carbine.
Karabinerfutteral	carbine bucket.
Karabinier-Regiment... ...	Carbineers (*cavalry regiment*).
Karbidlampe	acetylene lamp.
Karbol, Karbolsäure	carbolic acid.
Karbonsäure	carbonic acid.
Kardätsche	body-brush.
Kartätsche	case shot.
Karte	map.
Karten aufziehen	to mount maps.
Kartenvervollständigung ...	incorporation into maps.
Kartenzeichen...	conventional signs (*maps*).
Kartenzeichnen	map drawing.
Kartonzünder	cardboard (electric) fuze.
Kartusche	cartridge (*of gun*, not *rifle*).
Kartuschenbeutel	cartridge bag.
Kasematte	casemate.
Kasemattenlafette	casemate mounting.
Kaserne	barracks.
Kasernenarrest	confined to barracks.
Kasernenhof	barrack square.
Kasernenkrankenstube ...	regimental sick and inspection room.
Kasino	mess.
Kasinovorstand	mess president.

Kassation	cashiering, military degradation.
Kassieren	to cashier, dismiss.
Kasse	safe, money chest ; cashier's office.
Kassenabteilung	Finance section of the Intendance.
Kassendienst	pay department.
Kassenverwaltung	cashier's or paymaster's office ; financial administration.
Kassierer	cashier.
Kastenwagen	instrument wagon (fortress search-light section).
Kavallerie	cavalry.
Kavallerieattacke	cavalry charge.
Kavallerie-Division	Cavalry Division.
Kavalleriemassen	cavalry forces.
Kavallerieschleier	cavalry screen.
Kavallerie-Schützen	cavalry rifles (dismounted cavalry).
Kavallerie-Telegraphenschule	Cavalry Telegraph School.
Kavallerie-Telegraphenpatrouille.	cavalry telegraph patrol.
Kavallerie-Unteroffizier-Reitschule.	Cavalry Non-commissioned Officers' Riding School.
Kavallerist	cavalry soldier.
Kegelwinkel	angle of cone of dispersion (*of a shell*).
Kehle	throat ; gorge (*of a fort*).
Kehren	to turn about.
Kehrt !	About turn !
Keil	wedge, scotch.
Keilverschluss	wedge breech action (*of a Krupp gun*).
Keim	bud, embryo.
im Keime ersticken ...	to nip in the bud.
Kennbuchstabe	identification letter.
Kenntlich	conspicuous, clear, distinct.
Kenntnisnahme (zur) ...	" to note " (*at foot of orders*).
Kennwort	password.
Kennzeichen	distinguishing mark.
Kentern	to turn turtle.
Kern	kernel, core (*e.g., lead core of a bullet*).
Kernpunkt	strong point consisting of a fortified building or buildings.
Kerntruppen	picked troops.
Kernschussweite	point blank range.
Kessel	kettle, boiler.
Kettenbrücke	suspension bridge.
Keule	club, knobkerry.

Kies	...	...	...	gravel.
Kiesbettung	...	...	...	road ballast.
Kiesel	...	...	...	pebble.
Kieselguhr	...	...	...	"Kieselguhr" (*not translated; a fossil earth used as an absorbent for nitroglycerine in the manufacture of dynamite*).
Kieselstein	...	...	...	flint.
Kiesgrube	...	...	...	gravel pit.
Klammer	...	...	...	dog (*timber work*); bracket (*in printing, &c.*).
Klappbett	...	...	...	folding bed.
Klappe	...	...	...	jack (*telephone*).
Klappenschrank	...	...	indicator board (*telephone*).
Klappkragen	...	...	...	stand and fall collar (*tunic*).
Klebestreifen	...	...	...	adhesive tape (*of gas mask*).
Kleiftrupp (Kleiner-Flammenwerfer-Trupp).				small *Flammenwerfer* squad.
Klemme	...	...	...	terminal (*electrical*), binding screw.
Klemmen	...	...	...	to squeeze, jam.
Klemmer	...	...	...	riveter.
Klinge	...	...	...	blade (*of sword*).
Klingelausschalter	...	...	bell-push.
Klingelzeichen	...	...	...	bell signals.
Klopfanrichtung	...	...	mechanical dummy pick (*mining*).
Klopfschacht	...	...	...	inclined gallery in which a dummy pick is worked (*mining*).
Knagge	...	...	...	chock (*nailed on a baulk to prevent lashing from slipping*).
Knaggenbalken	...	...	chock baulks (*bridging*).
Knall	...	...	...	report.
Knallquecksilber	...	...	fulminate of mercury.
Knallsatz	...	...	...	detonating composition.
Knebel	...	...	...	toggles.
Kneifzange	...	...	...	pliers.
Kneifzange, schraubensichere				pliers, round-nosed pliers.
Knie	...	...	...	knee; salient.
Knopf	...	...	...	button.
Knotenpunkt	...	...	...	junction (*railways, &c.*).
Knüppel	...	...	...	club; winch.
Knüppel, Knüppelrost		...		baulk, round timber.
Knüppeldamm	...	...	corduroy road.
Kochgerät	...	...	...	cooking utensil.
Kochgeschirr	...	...	...	cooking utensil, mess tin.
Kochkessel	...	...	...	camp kettle.
Kochnische } Kochstelle }	...	...	cooking place.

Kofe	Commander of Telephone Troops (*at Army H.Q.*)
Kofl *or* Koflieg (Kommandeur der Fliegertruppen)	Commander of Aviation Troops (*with Army, Corps, &c.*).
Koflak (Kommandeur der Flug-Abwehr-Kanonen)	Commander of the Anti-aircraft Guns.
Kofu ... ... Kofunk	} Commander of Wireless Troops (*at Army H.Q.*)
Kogen-Luft (Kommandierender General der Luftstreitkräfte).	Commander of the Air Forces.
Kohldampf	hunger (*colloquial*).
Kohlenmonoxyd (Papier) ...	carbon monoxide (test-paper).
Kohlenoxyd	carbon monoxide.
Kohlensäure	carbonic acid.
Kokarde	cockade (*a circular metal badge, two of which are worn on the field service cap ; they show the Imperial (upper cockade) and State (lower cockade) colours in concentric rings*).
Kolben	butt (*rifle*).
Kolbenhals	small of the butt.
Kolbenbeschlag ⎫ Kolbenkappe ... ⎭	butt plate.
Kolonne	column.
Kolonnenbrücke	bridge for all arms.
Kolonnengebiet	back billeting area.
Kolonnenweg	track.
Kommandantur	Commandant's office.
Kommandeur	Commander.
Kommandieren	to detail, detach.
Kommandierender General ...	General Officer Commanding an Army Corps.
Kommandiert	man on detachment, attached (*e.g., to General Staff*).
Kommando	party, detachment, command; word of command. (*See also* Armee-Oberkommando.)
Kommandowort	word of command.
das Kommando führen ...	to be in command.
ein Kommando haben ...	to be on duty.
Kommiss	(*a prefix meaning army, e.g.,* " Kommissbrot," *army bread*).
Kommissäre (Auslade-) ...	detraining inspectors.
Kommissäre (besondere) ...	special inspectors.
Kommiss-Stiefel	ammunition boot.

Kompagnie	company.
Kompagnieführer	company commander.
Kompass	magnetic compass.
Königliche Dienstsache ...	on His Majesty's service.
Konserven	preserved food.
Konservenbüchse	preserved food tin.
Konserven-Verpflegung ...	tinned rations.
Konstatieren	to observe, find out ; to conclude.
Kontrolle	supervision, control.
Kontroll-Liste...	muster roll.
Kontrollschiessen	checking registration.
Kontroll-Versammlung ...	muster of reserves.
Kopfbedeckung	head-dress.
Kopffernhörer	head-receiver (telephone).
Kopframpe	end-loading ramp.
Kopfringscheibe	head target with rings (musketry).
Kopfscheibe	head target (musketry).
Kopfschützer	Balaclava helmet.
Kopfstück	top sill of a frame (mining).
Kopf-Zünder	nose fuze.
Koppel	belt.
Koppelschloss	belt buckle.
Koppelzeug	belt.
Korn	foresight of a rifle.
feines Korn	fine sight.
gestrichenes Korn	medium sight.
volles Korn	full sight.
Körperpflege	personal cleanliness.
Körperstrafe	corporal punishment.
Korporalschaft	section (¼ of a " Zug " consists of 2 " Gruppen," i.e., 18 men under an under-officer).
Korps	Corps.
Korps-Apotheker	Corps Apothecary.
Korpsarzt	Director of Medical Services (with Corps).
Korpsbrückentrain	Corps bridging train.
Korps-Intendant	Corps Intendant.
Korps-Intendantur	Intendance of the Corps.
Korps (-Ober) -Auditeur ...	Corps (Chief) Judge-Advocate.
Korps-Stabsveterinär ...	Major (veterinary).
Korpstagesbefehl	Corps order of the day.
Korpstelegraphenabteilung ...	Corps telegraph detachment.
Korrektur	correction.
Korridorgraben	gangway trench.
Kost	food.
Kosten	expenses.

Kot	mud, mire ; excreta.
Kräfte	forces, effectives.
Kräfteverteilung	distribution of forces, order of battle.
Kraftfahrbataillon	mechanical transport battalion.
Kraftfahrrad	motor bicycle.
Kraftfahrtruppen	mechanical transport troops.
Kraftfahrwesen	mechanical transport service.
Kraftlastwagen	mechanical transport lorry.
Kraftradfahrer	motor cyclist.
Kraftwagen	motor lorry.
Kraftwagengeschütz	anti-aircraft gun on motor lorry.
Kraftwagenkolonne	mechanical transport column.
Kraftwagenpark	mechanical transport park.
Kraftwagenstaffel	lorry train.
Kragen	collar.
Klappkragen	stand and fall collar.
Stehkragen	stand up collar.
Kragenpatten	collar patches.
Krankenlager	field dressing station.
Krankenliste	sick list.
Krankenkraftwagen	motor ambulance.
Krankenlöhnung	sick pay, pay while in hospital.
Krankenpflege (freiwillige) ...	voluntary aid.
Krankensammelpunkt ... Krankensammelstelle ...	collecting station (for wounded).
Krankenstube	dressing station.
Krankentrage	stretcher.
Krankenträger	stretcher-bearer.
Krankentransport-Abteilung	sick and wounded transport detachment, ambulance section.
Krankenwärter	hospital orderly, sick attendant.
Krankenwagen	ambulance wagon.
Krankenzug	ordinary train for sick and wounded.
Kratzhacke	long scraper.
Kreis (Kr in a postmark) ...	district.
Kreisbeamte	district official.
Kreisen	to move in a circle, circle (of aeroplanes).
Kreisleitung	omnibus circuit (electrical).
Krepieren	to explode (of shells) ; to die (of animals).
Kreuz	cross gallery (mining).
Kreuz (eisernes)	Iron Cross.
Kreuzfeuer	cross fire.
Kreuzhacke	pickaxe.
Kreuzmuffe	3-way joint (electrical).

Kreuzstelle	...	junction (*of roads, &c.*)
Kreuzung	...	crossing.
Kriegerverein ...	...	Military Veterans' Society.
Kriegs-Akademie ...	...	Staff College.
Kriegs-Akademiker ...	...	Staff College graduate
Kriegsamt	...	War Bureau.
Kriegsanruf	... } call to arms.
Kriegsaufgebot ...	... }
Kriegsausrüstung ...	...	war equipment.
Kriegsbedarf	...	military stores.
Kriegsbehörde ...	...	military authorities.
Kriegsbekleidungsamt	...	War Clothing Depôt.
Kriegsbereitschaft ...	...	readiness for war.
Kriegsbericht ...	...	war record, communiqué.
Kriegsberichterstatter	...	war correspondent.
Kriegsdienst	...	active military service.
Kriegsdienstipflichtiger	...	conscript.
Kriegsdrangsal ...	...	horrors of war.
Kriegsetat	...	war footing.
Kriegsfähig	...	fit for field service.
Kriegsfreiwilliger ...	...	war-volunteer.
Kriegsführung ...	...	conduct of war.
Kriegsfuss (auf—setzen)	...	to mobilize.
Kriegsgefangener ...	...	prisoner of war.
Kriegsgerät	...	war stores, war equipment.
Kriegsgericht	...	district court martial.
Kriegsgerichtsrat ...	...	Judge-Advocate-General.
Kriegsgesetz	...	martial law.
Kriegsgliederung ...	...	order of battle.
Kriegshilfsdienst ...	...	auxiliary service in war-time.
Kriegshund	...	war dog.
Kriegskunde	...	the art of war.
Kriegskunst	...	strategy, art of war.
Kriegslazarett (Abteilung)	...	clearing hospital (detachment).
Kriegslist	...	stratagem.
Kriegsmarsch	...	tactical march.
Kriegsministerium ...	...	War Ministry.
Kriegsministeriumserlass	...	War Ministry order.
Kriegsnot	...	stress of war.
Kriegsportion	...	field service ration.
Kriegsrat	...	council of war.
Kriegsrecht	...	martial law.
Kriegsschauplatz ...	...	theatre of operations *or* front.
Kriegsschule	...	War School (*somewhat similar to the R.M.C. Sandhurst and R.M.A. Woolwich*).
Kriegsstammrolle ...	...	nominal roll.

Kriegsstand	war strength, establishment.
Kriegstagebuch	war diary.
Kriegstark	at war establishment.
Kriegsverpflegungsamt	commissariat.
Kriegsverwaltung	war administration.
Kriegsvollbahn	normal gauge military railway.
Kriegswesen	military affairs, war department.
Kriegszahlamt	army pay office.
Kriegszahlmeister	army paymaster.
Kriegszufälle	contingencies of war.
Kroki	sketch map.
Krümper	cast horse kept on for fatigues.
Kruppe	crupper.
Kübel	bucket, pail.
Kugel	bullet, ball.
Kugelfest	bullet-proof.
Kugelhandgranate	ball hand grenade.
Kugellager	bearing block, ball bearing.
Kugelmine	spherical trench mortar shell.
Kugel, schwebende	parachute flare.
Kugelsicher	bullet-proof.
Kühler	water-jacket.
Kumt	collar (harness).
Kunde	news, note, intelligence.
Kundschaft	scouting, espionage.
Kundschafter	scout.
Kunstbauten	bridges, tunnels, &c.
Künsteleien	artificial methods.
Kupferleitungsdraht	copper line wire.
Kuppe	round hill-top, knoll.
Kuppel	cupola.
Kuppeln	to couple.
Kürassier	cuirassier.
Kürassier-Regiment	cuirassier regiment.
Kurbel	crank.
Kurbelwelle	crank shaft.
Küste	coast.
Küsten-Haubitze	coast defence howitzer.
Küsten-Kanone	coast defence gun.
Küstenlafette	coast defence mounting.
Küsten-Mörser	coast defence mortar.
Küstenverteidigung	coast defence.
Küster	sacristan.

L.

Labeflasche	bottle of cordial (*medical*).
Labung...	refreshment, treatment.
Ladefähig	in serviceable condition (*of ammunition*).
Ladehemmung	jam (*e.g., in rifle or machine gun*).
Ladekammer	chamber (*mining*).
Ausarbeiten der Ladekammer.	chambering.
Ladekommando	battery charging detachment (*wireless*).
Ladestelle	entraining station, loading platform.
Ladestock	ram rod.
Ladestörung	jam (*e.g., in machine gun*).
Ladestreifen	charger *or* strip (*for loading magazine rifle*).
Ladung...	charge.
geballte Ladung	concentrated charge.
eine kleine Ladung sprengen	to blow a camouflet.
Ladungsabstand	L.L.R. *or* line of least resistance (*mining*).
Ladungshülle	canister bomb (*used with light "Ladungswerfer"*).
Ladungsmine (Wurfladung) ...	canister bomb (*used with heavy "Ladungswerfer"*).
Ladungswerfer	"Ladungswerfer" (*not translated; a form of trench mortar*).
Lafette	gun carriage.
Kasemattenlafette	casemate mounting.
Küstenlafette	coast defence mounting.
Panzerlafette	shielded mounting.
Schirmlafette	carriage with overhead shield.
Unterlafette...	lower carriage.
Lafettenschwanz	trail (*of gun*).
Lafettensitze	seat on gun carriage.
Lafettensporn	spade of gun carriage, trail spade.
Lafettenwand	bracket of gun carriage.
Lage	situation, state of affairs, condition, state, position; fall (*of shell, &c..*)
Lager	camp.
Lager aufheben	to strike camp.
Lager aufschlagen	to pitch camp.
Lagerpfahl	picket post.
Lagerplatte	platform.
Lagerplatz	depôt, dump.

Lagerstroh	straw for bedding.
Lagerung	storage.
Lähmen	to disable, paralyze, neutralize.
Lahmlegung	silencing *or* neutralizing (*of artillery, &c.*).
Landbrücke	abutment.
Landesaufnahme	Survey Department (*of War Ministry*).
Landesfahrzeug	country cart.
Landgendarmerie	territorial police (Prussia).
Landjägerkorps	territorial police (Württemberg).
Landkarte	map.
Landmacht	land forces.
Landmine	land mine.
Landsturm	" Landsturm " (*not translated*).
Landsturmmann (gedienter)...	trained Landsturm man.
Landsturmmann (ungedienter)	untrained Landsturm man.
Landung	landing.
Landwehr	" Landwehr " (*not translated*).
Länge von Greenwich ...	longitude of Greenwich.
Längenabweichungen ...	errors in range.
Längenstreuung	errors in range due to the gun.
Langgranate	long shell.
Längsbestreichung ⎫ Längsfeuer ... ⎭ ...	enfilade fire.
Lanz	" Lanz " (*the name of a certain kind of trench mortar*).
Lappen	rag.
Fusslappen	foot bandage.
Lastkraftwagen	motor lorry.
Lasttier	pack animal.
Laterne	lantern.
Latte	lath.
Lattenröste	gratings, " duck boards."
Lattensteg	ladder bridge (*for crossing obstacles*).
Lauerstellung	position of readiness (*artillery*).
Lanze	lance.
Stahlrohrlanze	steel lance.
Lanzen zur Attacke gefällt ...	lances at the ready.
Lauf	course, run ; barrel (*of rifle*)
Laufbretter	" duck boards."
Laufbrücke	light bridge.
Laufbrücke (verstärkte) ...	light bridge, suitable for field artillery.
Laufen	to run.
Laufend	current.
auf dem Laufenden halten	to keep up-to-date (*e.g., a list*).

Läufer	runner (*messenger*).
Lauffeuer	running fire.
Laufgraben	communication trench.
Laufgrabendepot	trench depôt.
Laufgraben-Offizier	orderly officer in the trenches.
Laufschiene	guide-rail (*bridging*).
Laufschritt	double time.
Lauschposten	listening post.
Lautverstärker	amplifier valve (*telegraphy*).
Lazarett	hospital.
Lazarettabteilung	hospital section of the Intendance.
Lazarettgehilfe	hospital assistant.
Lazarett-Inspektor	Inspector of Hospitals.
Lazarett-Ökonomie-Verwaltung	hospital administration officials.
Lazarettschiff	hospital ship.
Lazarettwagen	ambulance wagon.
Lazarettzug	ambulance train.
Lebensbedingungen	conditions of living.
Lebensmittel	food.
Lebensmitteldepot	ration dump.
Lebensmittelempfänger ...	supply orderly.
Lebensmittelkiste	ration box.
Lebensmittelwagen	supply wagon.
Lebhaft	vigorous, rapid (*of firing*).
Lederring	} leather washer.
Lederscheibe	
Leeren	to empty, *sometimes* to deflate.
Lehm	clay.
Lehmboden	clay soil.
Lehmgrube	clay pit.
Lehr-Batterie	instructional battery.
Lehr-Regiment	instructional regiment
Lehrschmied	instructional forge.
Leibgarde der Hartschiere ...	Bavarian Bodyguard of Halbardiers.
Leibgendarmerie	Body Guard Police.
Leibgrenadier-Regiment ...	Body Grenadier Regiment.
Leibriemen	belt.
Leibwache	life guard.
Leichtatmer	low resistance breathing drum (*gas*).
Leichte Munitions-Kolonne ...	light ammunition column.
Leichte Nebelmine	light smoke-bomb.
Leichter Maschinen-Gewehr-Trupp.	light machine gun section.
Leichtkranken-Abteilung ...	section for mild cases.
Leichtverwundeten-Sammelplatz.	collecting station for slightly wounded.

Leistung	performance, work.
Leistungsfähigkeit	efficiency.
Leiten	to direct.
einheitlich leiten	to co-ordinate.
Leiterbrücke	ladder bridge.
Leitfeuer	slow match, safety fuze (mining, &c.).
Leitung	line, circuit (e.g., of telephone); command.
Hin- und Rückleitung ...	complete metallic circuit.
Leitungsdraht...	line wire, wire.
Leitungsgraben ...	telephone line trench.
Leitungskontrollieren... ...	line testing.
Leitungsnetz	telephone system.
Leitungspatrouille (Mann) ...	line man.
Leitungsprobe...	line test.
Leitungsprüfer	testing apparatus (electrical).
Leitungsschnur	lead.
Leitungszeicher	galvanometer.
Leitwelle	cam.
Lenkballon	dirigible airship.
Lenken	to guide, direct (fire).
Lenkluftschiff	dirigible airship.
Leuchtapparat ...	illuminating apparatus.
Leuchtgerät	
Leuchtgeschoss	star shell.
Leuchtkugel	light, light ball.
Leuchtmasse	phosphorescent compound.
Leuchtpatrone ...	light-pistol cartridge.
Leuchtpatronensignal ...	light-signal.
Leuchtpistole	light-pistol, illuminating pistol.
Leuchtrakete	light rocket.
Fallschirmrakete	parachute light.
Leuchtzeichen	light-signal.
Leuchtzeichen-Zwischenposten	light-signal station.
Leukoplast	adhesive tape.
Leutnant	Second-lieutenant.
Libelle	clinometer, level.
Libellenaufsatz	clinometer sight.
Libellenstück	level.
Libellenteil	clinometer graduation.
Lichtbildergerät	photographic apparatus.
Lichtkegel	beam (of searchlight).
Lichtsignalapparat ...	light-signalling apparatus.
Lichtsignale	luminous signals.
Lichtsignaltrupp	light-signalling detachment.

Lichtung	clearing (*e.g., in a wood*).
Lichtzentrale	light and power station.
Liebesgaben	gifts to soldiers in the field, " comforts."
Lieferant	contractor.
Lieferung	supply, delivery.
Liegen	" fall " (*e.g., of shell*).
Liegen, richtig	to be accurate (*e.g., of artillery fire*).
Liegeraum	small shelter for cover, lying.
Liegestütz	lying *or* prone position.
Linie	line.
Linie, erste, zweite, &c. ...	1st, 2nd, &c., Line Position.
vorderste Linie	front *or* foremost line.
Linienführung (festlegen) ...	to mark out.
Linien-Kommandantur ...	Office of Line Commandant (*railway*).
Links um !	Left turn !
Links schwenkt !	Left wheel !
List	stratagem, trick, ruse.
Liste	list, roll.
Litewka	" Litewka " *or* loose blouse.
Litze	braiding.
Lochmannhindernis	Lochmann entanglement.
Lockern (sich)	to become loose.
Löhnung	pay (*of soldiers*).
Lose (Schützenlinie) ...	thin *or* extended (line of skirmishers).
Lösung...	solution (*cipher*).
Losung... | Losungswort \}	countersign.
Lücke	gap.
Luft	air.
wir bekamen dicke Luft ...	we were heavily shelled (*colloquial*).
Luftangriff	aerial attack.
Luftdruck	air pressure.
Luftdruckwirkung	effect of concussion.
Lufterkundung	aerial reconnaissance.
Luftpumpe	air pump.
Luftrohrentzündung	bronchitis.
Luftschiff	airship.
Luftschiffahrt	aeronautics, airship voyage.
Luftschiffer	aeronaut.
Luftschiffer-Abteilung (Feld-)	balloon detachment.
Luftschiffer-Bataillon ...	air battalion.
Luftschiffführer	airship commander.
Luftschiffer-Trupp	airship detachment.
Luftschiffertruppen	airship and balloon troops.
Luftschraube	aeroplane (airship) propeller.

Luftschütz !	...	...	...	Air protection ! (*word passed down the telephone when hostile aircraft cross the line*).
Luftstreitkräfte		...	...	air forces.
Lunte ...	...	...	...	match (*mining, &c.*).

M.

Magazin	magazine, store, depôt.
Magazinfuhrparkkolonne	depôt supply park.
Magazinportion ...	regulation ration.
Magazin-Verwaltung ...	magazine officials.
Major	Major.
Mannschaft (arbeitende)	working party.
Mannschaften	rank and file, details.
Mannszucht	military discipline.
Manöver	manœuvre.
Mantel	greatcoat ; jacket (of gun, &c.).
Mantel-Kanone	jacketed gun.
Mantelriemen	greatcoat strap.
Marine	Navy.
Marine-Alarm-Signal ...	naval alarm signal (probably some form of mechanical fog signal).
Marine-Division (Brigade, &c.)	Naval Division (Brigade, &c.).
Marine-Infanterie-Regiment...	marine infantry regiment.
Marine-Korps	Naval Corps.
Marine-Landflieger-Abteilung	naval land flight (aviation unit).
Marketender	canteen personnel.
Marketenderei	canteen.
Marketenderwagen	canteen cart.
Markierter Feind	a " marked " enemy.
Marschbefehl	march orders.
Marschbereit	ready to move.
Marschfähig	able to walk, fit for marching.
Marschgeschwindigkeit ...	rate of marching.
Marschieren	to march.
Marschkolonne	infantry in fours, column on the march, column of route.
Marschleistung	marching power.
Marsch ! Marsch !	Double !
Marsch ohne Tritt	the break step.
Marschordnung	order of march.
Marschzucht	march discipline.
Maschinen-Flug - Abwehr-Kanonen-Zug.	anti-aircraft machine gun section.
Maschinen-Gewehr	machine gun.
Maschinen-Gewehr-Abteilung	machine gun detachment.
Maschinen - Gewehr - Ergänzungs-Zug.	machine gun section.
Maschinen-Gewehr-Kompagnie	machine gun company.
Maschinen - Gewehr - Scharfschützen-Kompagnie.	machine gun marksman company.

Maschinen - Gewehr - Scharf-schützen-Trupp.	machine gun marksman section (*obsolete*).
Maschinen-Gewehr-Stand ...	machine gun emplacement.
Maschinen - Gewehr - Trupp (Leichter).	light machine gun section.
Maschinen-Gewehr-Zug ...	machine gun section.
Maske	gas mask.
Maskenstoff	fabric of a gas mask.
Maskieren	to mask, make invisible.
Maskierung	camouflage.
Mass	measurement.
Massenfeuer	concentrated fire (*e.g.*, *of artillery*).
Massenstreufeuer	intense distributed fire (*artillery*).
Massnahme	measure, disposition (*of troops*).
Mastfernrohrtrupp	mast periscope section.
Material	equipment, material.
Materialanforderung	indent for stores.
Materialiendepot	supply dump.
Materialienwagen	material wagon (*telegraph equipment*).
Massstab	scale, rule, ruler.
Matrose	sailor.
Matrosen-Regiment	" Matrosen " regiment.
Mauerung	revetment.
Mauerwerk	masonry.
Maul	muzzle.
Maulesel } Maultier }	mule.
Meldedienst	service of despatch riders, runners, &c.
Meldegänger	runner.
Meldeheft	message book, report book.
Meldehund	messenger dog.
Meldekarte	message form.
Meldekette	chain of runners.
Meldeläufer	runner.
Meldeläuferkette	chain of runners.
Melden	to report.
Meldereiter	mounted orderly.
Meldesammelstelle	report centre.
Meldeverkehr	messenger traffic.
Meldewesen	Signals.
Meldung	report.
eine Meldung auffangen ...	to intercept a message.
Membrane	diaphragm.
Merkblatt	instructions, pamphlet.
Messbild	scale drawing.
Messingkartusche	brass cartridge case.

Messingklemme	brass terminal.
Messkette	measuring chain.
Messplan	artillery plan, " plan directeur."
Messplan-Abteilung	survey section (obsolete).
Messstäbe	scales (for stadia rods).
Messstelle	survey post or station.
Haupt-Messstelle	central compiling and plotting station.
Messtisch	plane table.
Messtrupp	survey station.
Messverfahren, akustisches ...	sound ranging.
Messzentrale	central survey office (compiling and plotting station).
Miete	shock, stook, rick, haystack.
Mikrophon	microphone.
Milchschmeisserei	light bombardment (colloquial).
Militär-Bäcker...	military baker.
Militär-Bau-Verwaltung ...	Military Works Administration.
Militär-Bau-Wesen	Military Works Department.
Militär-Eisenbahn-Direktion...	Military Railways Directorate.
Militär-Eisenbahn-Werkstätten-Amt.	Military Railway Workshop Office.
Militärfahrplan	military time table.
Militär-Flugwesen	Military Aviation Service.
Militär-Geistlicher	military chaplain.
Militär-Gerichts-Aktuar ...	military actuary.
Militär-Krankenwärter ...	sick attendant.
Militär-Küster	military sacristan.
Militärmass	military standard.
Militär - Pharmaceutisches-Personal.	military apothecaries.
Militär-Reit-Institut	School of Military Equitation.
Militär-Strafgesetzbuch ...	Military Criminal Code.
Militär-Verkehrswesen ...	Military Communication Service.
Militärischer Richter	member of a court martial.
Mine	mine or Minenwerfer shell.
Minenfeld	minefield.
Minenfeuer	Minenwerfer or trench mortar fire.
Minengalerie	gallery (mining).
Minengang	
Minengerbe	inverted cone in ground formed by firing a mine.
Minengraben	mine trench (in which entrances to mines are made).
Minenhalle	mine dug-out (mining).
Minenhülle	canister bomb (used with heavy " Ladungswerfer").

Minenhunde	truck (*mining*).
Minenkratze	clay adze (*mining*).
Minensperre	minefield.
Minensplitter	trench mortar bomb splinter.
Minensprengung	mine explosion, blowing of a mine.
Minenstollen	mine gallery.
Minentrichter	mine crater.
Minenwerfer	" Minenwerfer " (*usually not translated*) ; trench mortar.
Minenwerfer-Abteilung ...	*Minenwerfer* detachment (*obsolete*).
Minenwerfer-Bataillon ...	*Minenwerfer* battalion.
Minenwerfer-Kompagnie ...	*Minenwerfer* company.
Minenwerfer-Trupp	*Minenwerfer* sub-section (*crew for* 1 trench mortar).
Minenwerfer-Zug	*Minenwerfer* section (*sub-division of a " Minenwerfer " company*).
Mineur	miner.
Mineurkompagnie	mining company.
Minieren	to mine.
Missweisung der Magnetnadel	deviation of the compass.
Mithören	to overhear.
Mitteilung	message, report, information.
Mittelgang	central passage (*of* dug-out).
Mittelpferd	centre horse.
Mittelplatte	centre plate.
Mitwirkung	co-operation.
Mobil	mobile, mobilized.
Mobilisieren	to mobilize.
Mobilmachung	mobilization.
Mobilmachungsbefehl ...	mobilization order.
Monteur	mechanic (*Flying Troops*).
Montieren	to mount, to fit together.
Montierung	clothing, equipment ; mounting.
Montierungs-Depot-Verwaltung	clothing depôt officials.
Moritz	*name used to denote listening sets.*
Mörser	mortar.
Bronze-Mörser	bronze mortar.
Erdmörser	buried trench mortar, " earth mortar."
Küsten-Mörser	coast defence mortar.
Mörserbatterie...	mortar battery.
Morseschrift	Morse alphabet.
Motorwagen	motor car.
Mühle	mill.
Mulde	depression, hollow.
Mundloch	fuze hole.
Mundlochbüchse	old pattern type of fuze.

Mundlochfutter	gaine (*of fuze*).
Mundscheibe	mouth opening (*of a gas mask*).
Mundschlauch	mouth tube.
Mundstück	muzzle (*of gun*).
Mündung	mouth, muzzle.
Mündungsblitz	gun flash.
Mündungsdeckel	muzzle cap.
Mündungsfeuer	gun flash.
Mündungsfeuer anschneiden ...	to obtain bearings on the flashes.
Mündungsgeschwindigkeit ...	muzzle velocity.
Mündungsschoner	muzzle protector.
Munition	ammunition.
Alder B-Munition	" Alder B " ammunition (*explosive bullet for anti-aircraft purposes*).
gegurtete Munition... ...	filled belts (*machine gun*).
Grünkreuz-Munition ...,	" Green Cross " ammunition (*a form of gas shell*).
K-Munition	armour piercing ammunition (*rifle*) ; K-shell (*asphyxiating gas shell*).
L.E.-Munition	" L.E." ammunition (*explosive rifle bullets for anti-aircraft purposes*).
Panzer-Munition	armour piercing bullets.
S-Munition	" S " ammunition (*with the ordinary pointed rifle bullet*).
Spreng-Munition	the regulation explosive (*trinitrotoluol*).
T-Munition	T-shell (*lachrymatory gas shell*).
Munitionsausgabestelle ...	ammunition refilling point.
Munitionsbestand	stock of ammunition.
Munitionseinsatz	expenditure of ammunition.
Munitionsersatz	replenishment of ammunition.
Munitionskeller	deep dug-out for storing ammunition.
Munitionskolonne (Artillerie, Infanterie).	heavy ammunition column (artillery, infantry).
Munitionskolonne (leichte, leichte Feldhaubitze).	ammunition column (light, for light field howitzers).
Munitionsleute	ammunition party.
Munitionsnachschub	ammunition supply.
Munitionsniederlage	ammunition store.
Munitionsverbrauch	expenditure of ammunition.
Munitionsvergeudung ...	waste of ammunition.
Munitionswagen	ammunition wagon.
Munitionszug	ammunition train.
Muskete	automatic rifle.
Musketen-Bataillon	" Musketen " battalion (*armed with automatic rifles*).

Musketier	...	...	... private (*of the Active category in a line infantry regiment*).
Muster ...	...	...	... pattern.
Musterung	...	...	... mustering (*of recruits*), examination (*of recruits*).
Mütze ...	...	...	... cap.
Dienstmütze		...	... peaked cap.
Feldmütze		...	... field service cap.
Pelzmütze ...		...	... fur cap, hussar busby.
Schirmmütze		...	... peaked cap.

N.

Nachersatz	drafts.
Nachexerzieren	to do extra drill.
Nachfärben	to dye.
Nachforschung	investigation.
Nachfrage	inquiry, demand.
Nachhut ... ... Nachkommando ... }	rear guard.
Nachlieferung	supply.
Nachrichten-Abteilung ...	Intelligence Section.
Nachrichtenmittel	means of communication.·
Nachrichtenmittel-Offizier ...	communication officer.
Nachrichten-Offizier	Intelligence Officer.
Nachrichtensammlung ...	collection of intelligence.
Nachrichtensammelstelle ...	information centre.
Nachrichtenwesen	Intelligence Service.
Nachschub ...·	supply (of men and material, from rear to front), drafts, reinforcements.
Nachsehen	to inspect.
Nachsetzen (jemandem) ...	to pursue.
Nachspitzenkompagnie ...	rearward point company.
Nachtdienst	night shift.
Nachtrab	rear, rear guard.
Nachtrag	addendum, supplement (frequently met with in German orders).
Nachträgliche Überbauung ...	addition (i.e., which can be made to trenches).
Nachtrupp	rear party.
Nachuntersuchung (ärztliche)	2nd medical examination.
Nachwirkung	after effects (e.g., of gas).
Nachzügler	straggler, marauder.
Nähe	vicinity, nearness.
in erreichbarer Nähe ...	within striking distance.
Nahkampf	close combat.
Nahkampfgruppe	close-range group (artillery).
Nahkampfmittel	close-range weapons.
Namensanruf	roll call.
Namensverzeichnis	list of names.
Namenszug	regimental monogram.
Nasenklemme	nose-clip (gas).
Nasensteg	nose-piece (of goggles).
Nationale	details of birth, profession, &c (found in pay books and other official documents).

Nebel	mist, fog.
Nebelhorn	foghorn.
Nebelmine	smoke bomb.
Nebelwolke	smoke cloud.
Nebenabschnitt	neighbouring sector.
Nebenarm	minor branch of a branch gallery (*mining*).
Nebenfluss	tributary.
Nebengeleise	siding.
Nebenstrasse	} by-road, branch road.
Nebenweg	
Nebenwirkung...	secondary effect.
Neigung	inclination, slope.
Nervenschock	shell shock.
Nest	nest (*an isolated point secured in the enemy's line*).
Netz	network system.
Neuanlagen	new works.
Neuaufnahme	re-survey.
Neuer Art (n/A)	new pattern.
Neueingestellte	newly arrived men.
Neugestalten	to re-organize.
Neuigkeit	news.
Neutralitätsabzeichen ...	badge for neutrals.
Nichttransportfähig	unfit for transport.
Niederhalten	to dominate.
Niederkämpfen	to silence (*a battery*).
Niederkämpfung	silencing, neutralizing (*e.g., of hostile artillery*) ; counter-battery work.
Niederlage	defeat.
Niedermetzeln	to massacre, slaughter.
Niederschiessen	to shoot down.
Niederspannungsleitung ...	low tension line.
Niet	rivet.
Nische	recess (*e.g., in parapet or trench*).
Normalspurbahn	standard gauge railway.
Notbehelf	expedient ; emergency signal.
Notleitung	emergency line (*telephone, &c.*).
Notrampe	extemporised ramp (*for entraining purposes*).
Nottrage	emergency stretcher.
Notzeichen	emergency signal, S.O.S. signal.
Nullpunkt	zero, freezing point.
Nullpunkt (Batterie)	battery aiming point.
Nullzeit	zero time (*time for the commencement of an operation*).

O.

Oberarzt	Lieutenant (*medical*).
Oberbäcker	chief baker.
Oberbefehlshaber	Commander-in-Chief.
Oberfahnenschmied	farrier-serjeant.
Oberfeldheer	Supreme Commander-in-Chief (*i.e.*, the Emperor).
Ober-Festungs-Bauwärter ...	Chief Superintendent of Fortifications.
Oberfeuerwerker	chief artificer.
Oberfeuerwerkerschule ...	School for Artificers.
Obergefreiter	bombardier of foot artillery.
Obergeneralarzt und Sanitäts-Inspekteur.	Major-General (*medical*).
Obergurt	surcingle.
Oberhandwerker des Trains ...	chief tradesman of the Train.
Oberjäger	under-officer of rifles ; King's Messenger.
Oberkommando	Headquarters Staff.
Oberkommando (Armee-) ...	Army Headquarters.
Ober (Korps)-Auditeur ...	Chief (Corps) Judge-Advocate.
Oberlazarettgehilfe	chief hospital assistant.
Oberleutnant	Lieutenant.
Obermeister	Staff-serjeant of artillery technical establishments.
Oberquartiermeister	*not translated : Deputy Chief of the General Staff of an Army, or head of a section of the General Staff in the War Ministry.*
Erster-Oberquartiermeister	*not translated : Deputy Chief of the General Staff of the Field Army.*
Oberst	Colonel.
Oberstabsapotheker	chief apothecary.
Oberstabsarzt	Major (*medical*).
Oberstabsveterinär	brevet Major (*veterinary*).
Oberste Heeresleitung ...	Commander-in-Chief, General Headquarters, Higher Command.
Oberstleutnant	Lieutenant-Colonel.
Oberveterinär	Lieutenant (*veterinary*).
Oberwallmeister	staff-serjeant of fortifications.
Oberzündung (mit)	with overhead ignition (*pattern of 21 cm. mortar*).
Ofen	mine chamber (*mining*).

Offensive	offensive.
Offizier...	officer.
Offizier der Ronde ...	Officer of the Rounds, Visiting Rounds.
Offizier vom Tagesdienst ...	officer of the day.
Offizier-Aspirant	probationary or aspirant officer, cadet.
Offizier-Reitschule	Officers' Riding School (at Paderborn, Dresden, &c.).
Offiziersprüfung	officers' examination (examination for commission).
Offizierstellvertreter	acting officer (but usually not translated).
Ökonomie-Handwerker ...	regimental tradesman.
Öllappen	oily rags.
Ölspritzflasche...	oil can.
Operationsbasis	base of operations.
Operationsbefehl	operation order.
Operationsgebiet	zone of the field army.
O-Punkt	aiming point, reference point.
Ordnung (Tages-)	order of the day.
Ordnung (geschlossene) ...	close order.
Ordnung (offene)	open order.
Ordonnanz	orderly.
Ordonnanzdienst	orderly duty.
Ordonnanz-Offizier	orderly officer.
Organ	personnel; individual, subordinate, member of section.
Orientierung	orientation, reconnaissance.
Orientierung im Gelände ...	knowledge of the ground.
Orientierung	fire direction by means of prearranged light signals (artillery).
Ort	place, village.
Ort	in mining, used sometimes instead of " Spitze " for the face of a working.
Ortsbefehl	local order.
Ortsbehörde	municipal or local authorities.
Ortsbiwak	close billets.
Ortschaft	locality, village, place.
Ortsdienst	orderly officer's duty in place where troops are billeted.
Ortsfestungs - Flug - Abwehr-Kanonen-Zug.	anti-aircraft section attached to a fortress.
Ortskommandant	Town Major, local commandant. ·
Ortskommandantur	Town Major's office.
Ortskrankenstube	medical inspection room.
Ortslazarett	local hospital.

Ortsquartier ...	...	...	billet.
Ortsunterkunft	...	...	billets (*ordinary*).
Ortsvorstand ...	...	...	local authorities, mayor.
Ortsverkehr ...	...	...	local correspondence, traffic.
Öse	...	...	eye, shank, lug.

91

P.

Packtasche	wallet.
Packwagen	baggage wagon.
Paletot	greatcoat (*officer's*).
Pallasch	straight sword (*of heavy cavalry*).
Panjepferd	Russian horse (*requisitioned*).
Panjewagen	Russian cart (*requisitioned*).
Panzeraüto	armoured car, " tank."
Panzerbatterie	armoured battery.
Panzergranate...	armour-piercing shell.
Panzerkraftwagen	armoured car, " tank."
Panzerkuppel	armoured cupola.
Panzerlafette	shielded mounting.
Panzermunition	armour-piercing bullets.
Panzerplatte	armour plate.
Panzerschild	armoured shield.
Panzerturm	armoured turret.
Panzerwagen	armoured car, " tank."
Panzerzug	armoured train.
Paradeanzug	full dress.
Paradeschritt	" goose " step, drill step.
Parkieren	to park.
Park-Kompagnie	park company.
Parkplatz	park (*for ammunition, &c.*).
Parlamentär	bearer of a flag of truce.
Parole	countersign, parole.
Parolebuch	order book.
Parolelosung	countersign.
Pass	pass, permit, passport.
Patent	officer's commission.
Patrone	cartridge (*in the case of a gun, only when it is fixed ammunition*).
ungegurtete Patronen ...	loose rounds (*machine gun*).
Patronenhülse	cartridge case.
Patronenkasten	ammunition box.
Patronenlager	powder chamber.
Patronentasche	cartridge pouch.
Patronenwagen	small arms ammunition (S.A.A.) wagon.
Patrouille	patrol ; party.
Patrouillenangriff ... Patrouillengang ... Patrouillenunternehmung	} raid.
Patte	patch (*on lapel, sleeve, collar, &c.*).

Pauke	kettle drum.
Pauker	kettle drummer.
Pause (Feuer-)	pause *or* interval in firing.
in Pausen	intermittently.
Pechkranz	pitch ring (*for incendiary purposes*; *also used for indicating the line reached by troops*).
Pelerine	cape.
Pelzmütze	fur cap, hussar busby.
Perlen	" pearls " (*light-signal*).
Personal	personnel.
Pfadfinder	boy scout.
Pfahl	picket, pile.
Pfahlbrücke	pile bridge.
Pfahljoch	pile trestle.
Pfahlwerk	palisade.
Pfeil	arrow; picket; upright *or* leg (*mining*).
Pferd	horse.
Chargenpferd	officer's charger.
Dienstpferd	troop horse.
Handpferd	led horse.
Lastpferd	pack horse, heavy draught horse.
Mittelpferd	centre horse.
Reitpferd	riding horse.
Sattelpferd	saddle horse (*also* near horse)
Saumpferd	pack horse.
Stangenpferd	wheel horse.
Vorderpferd	lead horse.
Vorratspferd	spare horse.
Zugpferd	draught horse.
Pferdearzneikasten	veterinary chest.
Pferdeaushebungskommissar	horse requisitioning authority.
Pferdebahn	(40 *cm. gauge*) trench tramway (*animal traction*).
Pferdebestand	stock of horses.
Pferdedepot	remount depôt.
Pferdepflege	horsemastership.
Pferdeschutz	horse respirator (*gas*).
Pferdestall	stable (*for horses*).
Pferdetränken	watering horses.
Pferdewärter	groom.
Pferdezucht	horse breeding.
Pflichtvergessener	defaulter.
Pflock	peg, stake, picket.
Pflugschar	ploughshare.

Pfosten...	post, picket.
Phosgengas	phosgene gas.
Phosphor	phosphorus.
Photogrammetertrupp ...	photographic survey section.
Picke	pick, pickaxe.
Pickelhaube	spiked helmet.
Pickeln	to work with pickaxes.
Pilot	pilot (*aviation*).
Pinne	pivot.
Pionier...	pioneer, engineer.
Pionier-Abteilung	pioneer detachment.
Pionier-Belagerungs-Train ...	pioneer siege train.
Pioniergerät	pioneers' tools.
Pionier-Hauptdepot	pioneer main depôt.
Pionier-Kompagnie	pioneer company.
Pionier-Korps...	the Corps of Pioneers.
Pionierstand	pioneer dug-out.
Pistole	pistol.
gesicherte Pistole	pistol at safety.
Selbstladepistole	automatic pistol.
Pistolentasche	pouch.
Plänkler	skirmisher.
Planlosigkeit	want of method.
Planmässig	methodical, according to plan.
Planmaterial	topographical information, maps.
Planpause	tracing of a map.
Planquadrat	map square *or* co-ordinate (*on squared map*).
Planschiessen	shooting by the map (*artillery*).
Planwagen	ladder-sided wagon.
Platte	plate, platform.
Platzen	to burst (*of shrapnel*).
Platzpatrone	blank cartridge.
Plombe...	lead seal (*e.g., of gas mask drum*).
Polster	cushion.
Pontonbrücke...	pontoon bridge.
Pontonwagen	pontoon wagon.
Portepee	officer's sword-knot, *worn also by certain ranks* (*see below*).
Portepeeträger	*a rank which includes* " *Offizier-Stellvertreter*," "*Feldwebel*,"*"Vizefeldwebel*" *and some officials*.
Portion	ration for a man (*as opposed to* " *Ration* " *or forage ration*).
eiserne Portion	iron ration.
Kriegs-Portion	field service ration.
laufende Portion	ordinary ration.

Posten	sentry.
patrouillierende Posten ...	visiting patrols.
Posten ablösen	to relieve sentries.
Posten aufstellen	to post a sentry.
Posten stehen	to be on sentry duty.
Postenfeuer	infantry fire.
Postenhund	sentry dog.
Postenschüsse	infantry fire.
Postenstand	sentry post.
Postieren (sich)	to take up one's stand.
Postierung	sentry.
Post-Pferde und Wagen-Depot	post office horse and van depôt.
Poststempel	postmark.
Postwagen	postal van.
Postzeichen	postmark.
Prallschuss	ricochet.
Präsentiert das Gewehr ! ...	Present arms !
Präsenzstärke	(see " Friedenspräsenzstärke ").
Präzisionsschiessen	extremely accurate shooting.
Präzisionstelephon	detectophone.
Preisgeben	to abandon, give up.
Pressfutter	compressed forage.
Pressluftanlagen	air compressors.
Pressluftminenwerfer ...	pneumatic *Minenwerfer*.
Priester-Granate	Priester bomb (*fired from a " stick " bomb-thrower*).
Priester (Werfer)	Priester bomb-thrower.
Pritsche	bed (*of boards*).
Probe	test.
auf die Probe stellen ...	to test.
Probealarm	practice alarm.
Probeschuss	trial shot.
Profil	profile.
Progressivdrall	increasing twist.
Protze	limber.
Protzachse	limber axle.
Protzhaken	limber hook.
Protzkasten	limber box.
Protzöse	trail eye.
Proviantamt	supply office *or* depôt.
Proviantkolonne	supply column.
Proviantlager	supply depôt.
Proviantmeister	director of a supply depôt.
Prüfung	test, examination.
Prügel	stick; *also used for* code *or* cipher key.
Pulswärmer	wristlet.

Pulver	...	powder (*usually black powder*).
rauchloses Pulver ...	...⎫	smokeless powder.
rauchschwaches Pulver	...⎭	
Schwarzpulver ...	...	black powder.
Pulverfabrik	...	˙powder factory.
Pulverladung	...	charge of black powder.
Pulversatz	...	powder train.
Pulvertreibladung ...	...	propelling charge of black powder.
Pumpe	...	pump.
Punkt ˙...	...	point, full stop.
Punkt (im Gelände)	...	topographical feature.
O-Punkt	...	aiming point.
Punktnetz	...	skeleton (*triangulation*).
Punktschiessen ...	...	fire directed on a single point.
Puppen...	...	dummies.
Putzen	...	to clean, groom.
Putzlappen	...	cleaning rags.
Putzwerg	...	tow for cleaning, waste.
Putzzeug	...	cleaning materials.

Q.

Quadrat	...	...	square (*on squared map*).
Quadratmeter	...	...	square metre.
Quadratnetz	...	...	square (*on squared map*).
Quartier	...	...	billet, quarters.
Quartiermacher		...	officer *or* N.C.O. in charge of billeting party.
Quartiermeister	...	...	quartermaster.
Quartierwechsel	...	...	change of billeting area *or* quarters.
Quartierwirt	...	...	inhabitant on whom troops are billeted.
Quartierzettel	...	...	billeting paper.
Quaste	...	...	tassel.
Quellbrunnen	...	...	fountain, well, spring.
Quellenmässig	...	...	on good authority, authentic.
Quellgrund	...	...	ground full of springs, quagmire.
Quer	...	...	oblique, across.
Quer ab	...	...	abreast of.
Querbalken	...	...	bar, cross beam.
Querbolzen	...	...	cross bolt.
Querhindernis	...	...	obstacle perpendicular to the front
Querschnitt	...	...	profile or section (*e.g., of trench*).
Querstollen	...	...	transverse gallery (*mining*).
Querstrasse	...	...	cross road.
Quetsche	...	...	tool for crushing or squeezing.
Quetschen	...	...	to blow in (*mining*).
Quetschladung	...	...	⎫
Quetschmine	...	...	⎬ camouflet.
Quetschung	...	...	⎭

R.

Rabatte	plastron (*lancers*).
Radau	row, noise, shouting (*colloquial*).
Radfahrer	cyclist.
Radfahrerbataillon ...	cyclist battalion.
Radfahrerkompagnie	cyclist company.
Rahmen	frame, case.
Rahmenmaske... ...	frame mask (*gas mask, with special type of edging*).
Rakete	rocket.
Rampe	ramp, slope.
Kopframpe	end-loading ramp.
Notrampe	extemporised ramp.
Seitenrampe	side-loading ramp.
Rand	edge, rim *or* lip (*of crater*).
Rang	rank, grade.
Rangabzeichen	badges of rank.
Rangieren	to shunt (*railway*).
Rangliste	army list.
Rangstufen	degrees of rank, grades.
Rasen	sods, turf.
Rasenabdeckung ...	⎫
Rasenplacke	⎬ layer of sods.
Rasenstück	sod.
Rast	halt, rest, stay.
Rat	councillor ; advice, council.
Ration	forage ration (*as opposed to " Portion," or ration for man*).
Rations-Sätze	scale of rations.
Raubzug	marauding raid.
Rauchlos	smokeless (*powder*).
Rauchrakete	smoke rocket.
Rauchschleier	smoke cloud *or* screen.
Rauchschwach	smokeless (*powder*).
Raum	space, frontage, room.
Rauchschwaden	smoke clouds.
Räude	mange.
Räumen	to evacuate.
Raumlöffel	scoop, scraper (*mining*).
Räumung	evacuation.
Rechnungsfehler	miscalculation.
Rechts um kehrt !	About turn !
Rechts um !	Right turn !
Rechtwinkliger Trichter ...	two-lined crater (*mining*).
Rege	lively, active.
Regeln	to regulate, control.

Regiment	... regiment.
Regimentsbagage ...	... regimental transport.
Regimentsgefechtsstand	regimental battle H.Q.
(Stelle).	
Regimentskommandeur	... regimental commander.
Regimentsstab ...	... regimental staff.
Regimentsstapelplatz...	... regimental dump.
Regimeutstambour ...	... regimental drummer.
Reglement	... regulations, text book, manual.
Regler	... corrector.
Reglerkorrektur ...	... correction.
Reibsatz	... fulminate.
Reibzünder	... friction lighter.
Reibzündschraube ...	... friction tube.
Reichweite	... range.
Reih und Glied ...	... rank and file.
Reihen (in)	... in file.
Reihenfolge	... order of succession.
Reihenkolonne (in) ...	... in file.
Reisegebührnisse ⎱ ...	... travelling allowance.
Reisekosten ⎰	
Reisemarsch	... march route.
Reisequartier	... march billet.
Reisigbündel	... brushwood, fascine, fagot.
Reissleine	... lanyard.
Reitende Artillerie ...	... horse artillery.
Reitende Batterie ...	... horse artillery battery.
Reitendes-Feldjäger-Korps ...	... King's Messengers.
Reiter	... trooper, horseman.
Schwerer Reiter ...	... trooper (of heavy cavalry).
Reiter-Regiment, Schweres ...	... not translated; heavy cavalry regiment (Bavarian or Saxon).
Reithose	... pantaloons.
Reitpferd	... riding horse.
Reitzeug	... saddle and bridle.
Reizgeschoss	... gas shell, tear shell, lachrymatory shell.
Reizpatrone	... gas cartridge (for testing gas masks).
Reizraum	... gas chamber (a room for testing gas masks).
Reizstoff	... irritant substance (lachrymator).
Reklamiert	... exempted, " combed."
Rekrutendepot ...	... recruit depôt.
Relais	... chain of men.
Relaisposten ...	... relay posts.
Relaisverbindung ...	... connecting files.
Remontedepot ...	... remount depôt.

Remontewesen	... ...	remount service.
Repartieren	... ...	to distribute.
Reserve	... ...	reserve.
Revier ...	... ...	barrack room (*sometimes*, medical inspection room).
Revier bekommen	... ...	to be put on the sick list.
Revierkranken	... ...	men who are sick (*light duty*).
Revierkrankenstube ...	...	regimental sick and inspection room.
Revolver	... ...	revolver.
Revolverkanone	... ...	revolver-gun.
Revolverkanonen-Abteilung...		revolver-gun detachment.
Revolvertrommel	... ...	cylinder of revolver.
Richtbaum	... ...	traversing lever (*on trail*).
Richtbogen	... ...	clinometer.
Richten	... ...	to lay (*a gun*).
Richtfläche	... ...	clinometer plane.
Richthebel	... ...	elevating lever.
Richtkanonier	... ...	gun layer.
Richtkreis	... ...	director (*gunnery*).
Richtkreisdiopter	... ...	" flash spotter."
Richtkreiskorrektur ...	...	corrections for displacement (*gunnery*).
Richtkreiszahlen	... ...	" director " readings.
Richtlatte	... ...	aiming post.
Richtmaschine	... ...	elevating or traversing handwheel.
Richtschraube	... ...	elevating screw.
Richtstäbchen	... ...	aiming post.
Riegel ...	... ...	bolt (*on door, &c.*); switch trench.
Riegelgraben ...	... ...	switch trench.
Riegelstellung	... ...	switch line.
Riemen...	... ...	strap, sling (*of rifle*).
Ringel ...	... ...	loop, coil.
Ringkanone (R.K.)	... ...	gun with chase rings.
Ringkragen	... ...	gorget.
Ringscheibe	... ...	ring target (*bull's eye target with rings*).
Rinne ...	... ...	gutter (*of trench*).
Rittmeister	... ...	Captain (*of cavalry or train*).
Rock ...	... ...	coat, jacket.
Waffenrock ...	... ...	tunic, field service jacket.
Rödelung	... ...	rack-lashing (*bridging*).
Rohr ...	... ...	bore ; gun (*artillery*).
Rohrbremse	... ...	buffer.
Rohrdetonierer	... ...	burst in the bore.
Röhrenleitung	... ...	pipe line.
Rohrhalter	... ...	breech lug.

D 2

Rohrjacke	jacket.
Rohrkrepierer	burst in the bore.
Rohrmündung	muzzle.
Rohrrücklauf	gun recoil.
Rohrrücklaufgeschütz ...	gun which recoils in its carriage.
Rohrwand	bore.
Rohrwagen	travelling carriage (*for* 21 *cm. mortar*).
Rohrwiege	cradle.
Rohrzerscheller ...	} burst in the bore.
Rohrzerspringer ...	
Rollbahn	trench tramway (50 *cm. gauge*).
Rolle	roll; pulley; rôle.
Rollwagen	lorry (*fortress searchlight section*).
Ronde	" Rounds."
Ronde-Offizier	Officer of the Rounds.
Rossarzt	veterinary surgeon.
Rost	trench boarding, " duck boards; " gridiron, grate.
Rösten	to roast.
Rosten	to rust.
Rote Kreuz, Das	the Red Cross.
Rotte	file.
blinde Rotte	blank file.
gerade Rotten	even files.
ungerade Rotten	odd files.
Rotz	glanders.
Rücken...	to march, move ; *also* back, rear.
Rückenfeuer	reverse fire.
Rückenwehr	parados.
Rückfahrt	return journey.
Rückleitung	return (*of electric circuit*).
Rückmarsch	march back, return march.
Rückmeldung	reply.
Rückschlag	defeat, reverse.
Rückstand	residue.
Rückstoss	repulse, recoil.
Rückwärtig	behind the lines, rearward, back, rear, retired.
Rückwärts	backwards, to the rear.
Rückzug	retreat, retirement.
Ruder	oar.
Steuerruder	rudder.
Ruf	shout, call, hail, cry ; reputation, repute.
Rufzeichen	call signal (*wireless*).
Ruhe	rest, calm, quiet.
Ruhebatallion	battalion resting.
Ruhelager	rest camp.

Ruhequartier ...	...	...	rest billets.
Ruhiges Feuer...	...	...	deliberate fire (*artillery*).
Rühren	...	...	to move.
Rührt Euch ! ...	...	...	Stand (or march) at ease !
Rundballon	...	...	spherical balloon.
Rundbild	...	...	panorama
Rundblickfernrohr	...	...	panorama sight.
Runde ...	...	...	" Rounds."
Russenwache ...	...	...	guard for Russian prisoners of war.
Rüsten	...	...	to prepare, equip, arm.
Rutschbahn	...	...	inclined plane for sliding material down, haulage apparatus (*mining*).
Rutschung	...	...	falling away of earth (*e.g.*, *in a trench*).

S.

Säbel	sabre (*mounted troops*).
Säbelgriff	sword grip.
Säbelklinge	sword blade.
Säbelkoppel	sword belt.
Säbelschlaufe	frog (*of a bayonet, &c.*).
Säbeltasche	sabretache.
Säbeltroddel	bayonet knot.
Sackgraben	block trench.
Säge	saw, saw edge (*of bayonet*).
Sägewerk	saw mill.
Salve	salvo (*artillery*), volley (*rifle*).
Salve abgeben	to fire a volley *or* salvo.
Salzdecke (*contraction for "Schutzsalzdecke"*).	anti-gas cover.
Salzsäure	hydrochloric acid.
Sammelkompagnie	salvage company.
Sammeln!	the "Assembly" (*infantry*).
Sammeln	to collect, rally, gather.
Sammelort	dump.
Sammelplatz	place of assembly, collecting station.
Sammel-Sanitäts-Depot ...	medical stores collecting station.
Sammelstation	} collecting station.
Sammelstelle	
Sandgrube	sand pit.
Sandsack	sandbag.
Sandsackunterlage	a pedestal built up of sandbags.
Sandschutzbrillen	sand goggles.
Sanitätsdienst	Army Medical Service.
Sanitätsinspektion	Medical Inspection.
Sanitätskasten	medical chest.
Sanitätskompagnie	bearer company, medical company.
Sanitätskorps	Medical Corps.
Sanitäts-Kraftwagen-Kolonne	motor ambulance convoy.
Sanitätsmannschaften ...	medical orderlies.
Sanitäts-Offizier	medical officer.
Sanitäts-Offizierdiensttuer ...	*retired medical officer holding appointment.*
Sanitätspersonal	medical personnel.
Sanitätssoldat	hospital orderly.
Sanitätsstaffel	bearer detachment.
Sanitätstasche	medical wallet.
Sanitätstornister	medical knapsack.
Sanitätsunterstand	field dressing station in a dug-out, medical dug-out.

Sanitätsverbandzeug	bandage, field dressing.
Sanitätsvorratwagen	medical store wagon.
Sanitätswagen	ambulance wagon.
Sanitätswesen	medical service.
Sappe	sap.
Sappenkopf	saphead.
Sappenposten	listening post in sap.
Sappenspitz	saphead.
Sattel	saddle.
Sattelbaum	saddle tree.
Satteldecke	saddle cloth.
Sattelgurt	girth.
Sattelknopf	pommel.
Sattelpferd	riding horse (*also* near horse).
Sattelseite	near side.
Satteltasche	saddlebag.
Sattelzeug	saddlery.
Sattler	saddler.
Satz	jump, bound ; ingredients, composition (*e.g.*, " *Zündsatz* " *or detonating composition*) ; sentence (*grammatical*).
Säuberung	clearing (*of trenches, &c.*).
Sauerstoff	oxygen.
Sauerstoffeinatmungsgerät ...	oxygen breathing (inhalation) apparatus.
Schablonieren	to stencil.
Schacht	shaft (*mining*).
Schachtel	packet (*e.g.*, *of cartridges ; 3 clips of 5*).
Schaffen	to create, construct, arrange ; to do, convey.
nach vorne schaffen ...	to carry to the front.
Schall	sound.
Schallmesstrupp	sound ranging section.
Schallmesszentrale	sound ranging central station.
Schallquelle	source of sound.
Schallrichten	sound ranging.
Schallsignal	sound signal.
Schallwellen	sound waves.
Schaltbrett	electrical switch board.
Schalter	switch.
ausschalten	to switch off.
einschalten	to switch on.
Schalthebel	switch.
Schandeck	gunwale (*pontoon*).
Schanzarbeiten	entrenching works.

D 4

Schanzbataillon	entrenching battalion.
Schanze	a field work.
Schanzen	to dig, entrench.
Schanzgeräte	entrenching tools.
Schanzkorb	gabion.
Schanzkorbbrücke	gabion bridge.
Schanztätigkeit	trenchwork, entrenching.
Schanz- und Werkzeugwagen	entrenching and tool wagon (*pioneers*).
Schanzzeug	entrenching tools.
Schanzzeugwagen	entrenching tool wagon (*infantry*).
Schapska	see " Tschapka."
Scharf	sharp; "live" (*of a grenade, &c.*).
Handgranate scharf machen	to insert a detonator in a grenade.
Scharfpatrone	ball cartridge.
Scharfschiessen	to fire with ball ammunition.
Scharfschiesser	sniper.
Scharfschütze	marksman, sniper.
Scharfschützenfeuer	independent fire.
Scharfschützen-Trupp (M.G.)	machine gun marksman section.
Scharmützel	skirmish.
Schärpe	officer's sash.
Scharte	fissure, gap; loophole, embrasure.
Schartenklappe	loophole shutter (*of infantry shield*).
Schartenplatte	loophole shutter.
Schartenschlitz	loophole.
Schartensohle	lower edge of loophole.
Schartenweite	width of loophole.
Schattenwirkung	shadow effect.
Schätzen	to judge (*distance*), estimate, value.
Schaufel	shovel.
Scheibe	target.
Brustscheibe	head and shoulders target.
Figurscheibe	figure target.
Kniescheibe	kneeling figure target.
Kopfscheibe...	head target.
Ringscheibe	ring target (*bull's eye target with rings*).
Scheide	scabbard.
Scheinangriff	feint attack.
Scheinanlage	dummy trench *or* defensive work.
Scheinbatterie	dummy battery.
Scheinbeobachter	dummy observer.
Scheinflankierung	dummy flanking position.
Scheingefecht	sham fight.
Scheinschulterwehr	dummy traverse.
Scheinstellung...	dummy position.

Scheinunternehmung	...	feint attack.
Scheinwerfer	...	searchlight.
Scheinwerferzug	... ...	searchlight section.
Scherenfernrohr	... ...	stereo-telescope, " scissors " telescope.
Halbschere	...	the half scissors (*represents half the " scissors " telescope*).
Schicht	...	shift (*mining, &c.*) ; course, layer.
Schutzschicht	... ...	protecting course (*roof of dug-out, &c.*).
Schichtlinie	...	contour.
Schiebbahn	...	trolley line.
Schiebkarren	...	wheelbarrow.
Schiebwagen	...	hand trolley.
Schiedsrichter	...	umpire.
Schiene	...	rail (*railway*).
Schienendecke... ...	...	layer of rails..
Schiessanweisung ...	...	instructions for gunnery or musketry.
Schiessbaumwolle ...	...	guncotton.
Schiessbeispiel ...	...	example of ranging.
Schiessbuch	...	*book containing record of the mark manship of an individual soldier.*
Schiessdienst	...	musketry duty.
Schiessen (beginnen, das)	...	to open fire.
Schiessfrei	...	out of range.
Schiessgerüst	...	stand (*for machine gun, &c.*).
Schiesslistenbuch	...	register of firing of a battery.
Schiessplatz	...	artillery range.
Schiessscharte	⎱	loophole.
Schiessschlitz	⎰	
Schiessschule	...	School of Musketry.
Schiessschule (Artillerie)	...	School of Gunnery.
Schiessstand	...	rifle range.
Schiesstafel	...	range table.
Schiessübung (jährliche)	...	annual musketry course.
Schiessverfahren ...	...	fire procedure, fire tactics.
Schiessverhau	...	barricade *or* abatis of trees.
Schiessvorschrift ...	...	regulations for gunnery or musketry.
Schiessweite (in) ...	...	within range.
Schiffbrücke	...	bridge of boats.
Schild	...	shield.
Schildbatterie	...	shielded battery.
Schildwache	...	sentry.
Schildwache aufstellen	...	to post a sentry.
Schirmlafette	...	overhead shield (*of gun*).
Schirmmütze	...	peaked cap.

Schirren	...	...	to harness.
Schirrmeister	...	...	storekeeper (N.C.O.).
Schlacht	...	...	battle.
Schlächterei	...	...	butchery.
Schlächtergeräte	...	...	butcher's implements.
Schlachtlinie	...	...	line of battle.
Schlagbolzen	...	...	striker (*e.g., in a breech mechanism*).
Schlagen	...	...	to strike, beat, defeat; throw (*a bridge*); to submit (*proposals*).
Schlagfeder	...	...	striker spring.
Schlagrohr	...	...	friction tube, friction igniter.
Schlagwort	...	...	code word.
Schlagzünder	...	...	percussion fuze.
Schlangenlinie	...	...	line with zig-zag trace.
Schlappe	...	...	reverse.
Schlauch	...	...	tube, hose.
Schleichen	...	...	to crawl, creep.
Schleichpatrouille	...	...	reconnoitring patrol.
Schleier	...	...	screen (*e.g., cavalry, smoke, &c.*).
Schleiflatte	...	...	} rubbing strakes (*pontoon*).
Schleifleisten	...	...	
Schlepparbeit	...	...	haulage work.
Schleppen	...	...	to haul, tow.
Schleppschacht	...	...	inclined gallery (*mining*).
Schlepptau	...	...	tow rope.
Schlepptrupp	...	...	hauling gang (*mining*).
Schleudergestell	...	...	catapult.
Schleudern	...	...	to throw by means of a catapult.
Schleuse	...	...	sluice, lock.
Schlinge	...	...	sling, noose, trap.
Schlitten	...	...	sledge (*e.g., of a machine gun*).
Schlitz	...	...	slit, notch.
Schloss	...	...	lock (*e.g., of door, rifle, &c.*); castle.
Schlösschen	...	...	cocking piece.
Schlossgarde-Kompagnie	...	Castle Guard.
Schlossschützer	...	...	lock shield *or* protector.
Schlossteile	...	...	breech mechanism.
Schlucht	...	...	ravine.
Schlüssel	...	...	key *or* spanner.
Schmal	...	...	narrow.
Schmalspurbahn	...	...	narrow gauge railway.
Schmiedewagen	...	...	forge wagon.
Schmieren	...	...	to grease.
Schnalle	...	...	buckle.
Schnallen	...	...	to buckle, strap.
Schneid	...	...	dash, smartness, spirit, energy.
Schneide	...	...	edge (*of a sword, &c.*).

Schneiden	to cut; to take bearings (*e.g.*, *in survey work*).
Schneider	tailor.
Schneidig	sharp, smart, energetic, vigorous.
Schnelldraht ... ... ⎱	portable wire entanglement; con-
Schnelldrahthindernis ⎰	certina wire entanglement.
Schnellfeuer	rapid fire.
Schnellfeuergeschütz	quick firing gun.
Schnellhindernis	ready made obstacle, emergency obstacle.
Schnelltelegraph	mechanical telegraph.
Schnellzündschnur	instantaneous fuze.
Schnitt	intersection, bearing.
Schnurbesatz	braid on hussar's tunic.
Schnurleine	small lashing.
Schnürschuhe	ankle boots, lace boots.
Schonen	to spare, preserve.
Schonungsbedürftige	*men who, it is considered, should not be employed in front line for various reasons, e.g., health, family reasons, &c.*
Schoss	skirt (*of a tunic*).
Schotter	road metal, ballast, broken stones.
Schraffieren	to hatch, hachure (*on a sketch*).
Schrägfeuer	oblique fire, flanking fire.
Schrapnell	shrapnel.
Schraubanker	screw anchor bolt (*for obstacles*).
Schraubenmutter	nut (*screw-threaded*).
Schraubenschlüssel	screw driver, spanner.
Schraubenzieher	screw driver.
Schraubpfahl	screw post (*for wire entangle-ment*).
Schreiber	clerk.
Schreibstube	orderly room, office.
Schritt	pace.
Schuh	shoe, boot.
Schulschiessen...	preliminary practices (*musketry, &c.*).
Schulterklappe	shoulder strap.
Schulterschnur	shoulder cord.
Schulterwehr	traverse.
Schuppe (*or* Schuppen) ...	shed, hangar.
Schurzholz	casing *as opposed to* " *Getriebholz*," *frame and sheeting or lagging (trenches and mining)*.
Schurzholznest	shelter.

Schuss	shot, "round," "rounds."
Bogenschuss	high angle fire.
Vereinzelte Schüsse ...	desultory fire.
Schuss !	Fire !
Schuss lag weit	" over."
Schuss lag kurz	" short." } (of results
Schuss lag gut im Ziel ...	" hit." } of firing).
Schussbereit	ready to fire.
Schussbeschädigung	damage caused by gunfire.
Schussfeld	field of fire.
Schussrichtung	line of fire.
Schusssicher	shell-proof (against continuous bombardment by 6-in. guns) (sometimes " bullet-proof ").
Schusstafel	range table.
Schussweite	range.
wirksame Schussweite ...	effective range.
Schusszahl	number of rounds.
Schütten	to heap up, dam.
Schutz	protection, cover.
Schutzbrille	smoked spectacles, goggles.
Schütze...	rifleman, sniper, marksman, private (in all machine-gun units and in " Schützen " battalions).
Schützenabzeichen	marksman's badge.
Schützenauftritt ... }	fire step.
Schützenbank ... }	
Schützenfeuer, langsames ...	deliberate fire.
Schützengefecht	skirmish.
Schützengraben	fire trench.
völlig eingeschnittener Schützengraben.	trench without parapet.
geschlossene Schützengräben	closed works.
Schützengraben-Kanonen-Abteilung.	trench-gun detachment.
Schützenhöhle	dug-out.
Schützenlinie	skirmishing line, extended order.
Schützenloch	rifle pit.
Schützennester	rifle pits.
Schützennische	recess (in parapet).
Schützenschleier	covering party.
Schützenstand...	rifle range.
Schutzgerät	defensive appliances.
Schutzmaske	anti-gas mask.
Schutzsalz	protective salts (anti-gas).
Schutzsalzdecke	anti-gas cover.
Schutzsalzlösung	protective salts solution (anti-gas).
Schutzschicht	protecting course (e.g., in roof of dug-out).

Schutzschild	armoured shield.
Schutzstaffel	protective flight (*aviation unit*).
Schutztruppen	The Protectorate Troops (*Colonies*
Schwalbennester	bandsman's epaulettes.
Schwanken	to fluctuate, vary ; to reel.
Schwanz (Lafettenschwanz) ...	trail.
Schwärmen	to extend (*line of skirmishers*).
Schwebebahn	suspension railway.
Schwefelkohlenstoff	carbon disulphide (*gas*).
Schwelle	threshold, sill ; sleeper, (*railway*).
Schwenken	to wheel.
Schwenkungswinkel	arc of traverse.
Schwere Artillerie des Feld-	Heavy Artillery of the Field Army.
heeres.	
Schwere (leichte) Feldhaubitz-	heavy (light) field howitzer battery.
batterie.	
Schwere Kolonnen-Brücke ...	heavy bridge for all arms.
Schwerer Reiter	trooper (*of heavy cavalry*).
Schwerer Rheinbrückentrain...	Heavy Rhine Bridging Train.
Schweres Reiter-Regiment ...	*not translated ; heavy cavalry regi-ment (Bavarian or Saxon)*.
Seebataillon	marine infantry battalion (*peace*).
Seeflieger-Abteilung	naval air (hydroplane) squadron.
Seele	soul ; bore (*of a gun, &c.*).
Seelendurchmesser ... ⎱	calibre.
Seelenweite ... ... ⎰	
Seewehr	" Seewehr " *or* naval reserve (*corresponds to* " *Landwehr* ").
Segeltuchtasche	canvas wallet.
Sehschlitz	observation loophole (*e.g., in a shield*).
Seitenabstand	displacement (*gunnery*).
Seitenabweichung	error in direction (*gunnery*).
Seitendeckung	flank guard.
Seitengewehr	side arm, bayonet.
Seitenrampe	side-loading ramp.
Seitenrichtmaschine	traversing gear.
Seitenschlag	branch gallery (*mining*).
Seitenstück	stanchion of a frame (*mining*).
Seitenstreuung	lateral error (*in the shooting of a gun*).
Seitenverschiebung	displacement (*artillery*).
Seitliche Wirkung	lateral effect.
Sektion	section.
Selbständig	independent, self reliant.
Selbstlader	automatic (*pistol*).
Selbstretter	life-saving apparatus, *similar to* " Salvo Set " ; oxygen breathing apparatus.

Senkloch	drain.
Senkrecht	vertical, perpendicular.
Senkschacht	vertical shaft.
Senkung	depression.
Sergeant	serjeant (*rarely used*).
Sergeantenknopf	*button* (*large*) *worn on collar as badge of rank for serjeant-majors, &c.*
Setzwage	field level (*mining*).
Seuchenlazarett	hospital for infectious diseases.
Sichergestellung	detailing (*of a man*).
Sicherheitsbesatzung ...	emergency garrison.
Sicherheitsdienst	service of protection.
Sichern, sicherstellen	to cover, protect ; place at " safe " (*of a rifle*).
Sicherung	protection, covering party ; safety catch (*on rifle*).
Sicherungsband	safety band (*of a grenade*).
Sicherungsfeder	safety spring.
Sicherungsflügel	protective flank.
Sicherungslinie	switch line.
Sicherungsriegel	switch trench.
Sieb	gauze.
Siebseite	gauze side (*of gas mask drum*).
Siegen	to be victorious.
Signalapparat	signalling apparatus.
Signalpatrone	light-signal cartridge.
Signaltrupp	signalling troop (*cavalry*).
Signatur	conventional sign (*topog.*).
Sitz	seat.
Sitzstufe	step (*of trench*).
Skizze	sketch.
Sohlbreite ... ... Sohlenbreite	} width at bottom (*e.g., of a trench*).
Sohle	sole (*of trench, &c.*).
Soldat	soldier, private.
Soldbuch	pay book.
Sollstand und Iststand ...	establishment and strength.
Sonderleitung	special circuit.
Sondiernadel ...	*iron rod, 3 ft. long, used when searching for land mines.*
Späher	scout.
Spähtrupps	special reporting detachments.
Spalte	split, crack ; column (*of a tabular statement*).
Spanische Reiter	" knife rests " (*wire entanglement*).
Spannen	to stretch, strain, bridge ; to cock (*a rifle*).

Spannung	tension, strain, anxiety, suspense.
Spanntau	span lashing (*bridging*).
Spannweite	span (*bridging*).
Spaten	spade.
Speiseträger	"food carrier."
Sperre	barricade, block.
Sperrfall	case calling for barrage fire.
Sperrfeuer	barrage, barrage fire, curtain fire.
Sperrfeuer anfordern	to request barrage fire.
Sperrfeuer ausführen	to form a barrage.
Sperrfeuer auslösen	to employ barrage fire, form a barrage, open barrage fire.
Sperrfeuer einsetzen	to begin, open barrage fire.
Sperrfeuer einstellen	to cease barrage fire.
Sperrfeuer verstärken	to intensify barrage fire.
Sperrfeuerposten	barrage sentry.
Sperrfeuerräume	barrage areas.
Sperrfeuersignal	signal for barrage fire.
Sperrfeuerskizze	barrage sketch plan (*sketch showing the arrangements for barrage fire*).
Sperrfeuerstreifen	barrage zone.
Sperrtrupp	blocking party.
Sperrung	barricade, blocking.
Spiegel	mirror, *sometimes* periscope; bull's-eye.
Spiegelapparat	periscope.
Spielmann	bandsman, musician.
Spielleute	bandsmen.
Spindel	pinion.
Spion	spy.
Spionage-Dienst	espionage service.
Spitze	face, head of a gallery (*mining*); point (*cavalry*); spike (*of helmet*).
Spitzenfahrer	lead driver (*artillery*).
Spitzenkompagnie	point company.
Splitter	splinter.
Splittersicher	splinter-proof.
Splitterwirkung	splinter effect, fragmentation.
Splitzmaschine	cutting machine.
Sporn	spur; spade (*on trail of gun*).
Spornrädchen	rowel (*of spur*).
Sprachrohr	speaking tube.
Sprechtrichter	mouthpiece of transmitter (*telephone*).
Spreize	strut (*mining*).
Sprengbuch	register of mine explosions (*mining*).

Sprengen	to blow up, fire a charge, to " blow " (*mining*).
Sprengfertig	ready for firing (*of a mine*).
Sprenggas	explosive gas.
Sprenggehe	radius of disturbance (*mining*).
Sprenggranate	high explosive (H.E.) shell.
Sprengherde	centre of disturbance caused by explosion of a mine.
Sprenghöhe	height of burst (*of a shell*).
Sprengkammer	mine chamber.
Sprengkapsel	detonator.
Sprengkörper	slab of explosive.
Sprengladung ... ... Sprengmasse	} explosive charge.
Sprengmine	*Minenwerfer* H.E. shell.
Ganze schwere Sprengmine	full-sized heavy *Minenwerfer* H.E. shell.
Halbe schwere Sprengmine	half-sized heavy *Minenwerfer* H.E. shell.
Viertel schwere Sprengmine	quarter-sized heavy *Minenwerfer* H.E. shell.
Leichte Sprengmine ...	light *Minenwerfer* H.E. shell.
Mittlere Sprengmine ...	medium *Minenwerfer* H.E. shell.
Sprengmunition	regulation explosive.
Sprengpatrone...	explosive charge.
Sprengpulver	blasting powder.
Sprengpunkt	burst (*of a shell*).
Sprengstoff	explosive.
Sprengstoffgehalt	bursting charge.
Sprengstücke	splinters.
Sprengtrichter	mine crater.
Sprengung	explosion, blow.
Sprengvorschrift	Demolition Manual.
Sprengweite	zone covered by the burst of a shell.
Sprengwirkung	explosive effect.
Spritze	squirt, syringe ; face (*mining*).
Spritzweite	spraying distance, range of spray (*of a " Flammenwerfer "*).
Springen	to jump, leap, spring.
Spruch	sentence (*legal*).
Sprungweise	by rushes (*of an advance*).
Spule	coil.
Spur	track, trace.
Spurweite	gauge (*railway*).
Stab	Staff, headquarters.
Stabsapotheker	apothecary.
Stabsarzt	Captain (*medical*).

Stabshoboist	band-serjeant.
Stabshornist	serjeant-bugler.
Stabs-Nachrichten-Abteilung	Headquarters communication section.
Stabsoffizier	field officer.
Stabsquartier	Headquarters.
Stabstrompeter	serjeant-trumpeter.
Stabsveterinär	Captain (*veterinary*).
Stabswache	staff guard *or* escort.
Stacheldraht	barbed wire.
Staffel	échelon, wagon line (*artillery*).
Staffelförmig aufstellen ...·	to form up in several lines.
Staffelgebiet	back billeting area.
Staffelstab	divisional train échelon.
Staffelweise	in échelon.
Stafette	despatch rider.
Stahlblech	steel plate.
Stahlblende	steel loophole plate.
Stahlguss	cast steel.
Stahlhelm	steel helmet.
Stahlrohrlanze...	steel lance.
Stahlmantel	steel jacket (*of a gun*).
Staken	boat hook.
Stalldienst	stable duty.
Stallleine ... ..: ...	picket line.
Stammrolle	register of recruits, nominal roll (*of a company, &c.*).
Stammrollenauszug	extract from the recruit register or nominal roll.
Stammrollenummer	serial number allotted to each man in a company.
Stand	employment ; state, condition, class.
in Stand setzen	to repair.
Standgericht	Regimental Court Martial (R.C.M.).
Standort	position, place where an individual or unit is quartered.
Standortswechsel	change of position, change of garrison.
Stange	pole.
Stangenpferd	wheel horse, wheeler.
Stangenvisier	tangent sight.
Stapeln	to pile up, stack (*shell, cartridges, &c.*).
Stapelplatz	depôt, dump, dumping place.
Stärke	strength, forces.
Stärkeausweis	return of fighting strength.

Stärkebestand...	actual strength.
Stärkeverhältnis	comparative strength.
Starkstrom-Abteilung ...	electrician detachment.
Starkstromanlage	electric power installation.
Stationsanruf	} station call (*wireless*).
Stationsruf	
Stativ	stand, tripod (*for telescope or camera*).
Steg	footpath, footbridge.
Stehende Heer (Das)	the Standing Army.
Steigbügel	stirrup iron.
Steigriemen	stirrup leather.
Steigung	gradient.
Steilbahngeschütz	howitzer.
Steilfeuer	high-angle fire.
Steilfeuergeschütz	howitzer.
Steinbruch	quarry.
Steinschlag	shower of stones.
Steinschotterung	road-metalling.
Stelle	position.
auf der Stelle treten ...	to mark time.
Stellen	to place ; to set (*a fuze*).
zur Verfügung stellen ...	to place at disposal.
Stellmacher	wheeler.
Stellmacherkasten	box of wheeler's tools.
Stellring	setting ring (*on time fuze*).
Stellschlüssel	fuze key.
Stellung	position ; line ; emplacement ; trenches.
erste, zweite Stellung ...	1st, 2nd line position.
verdeckte Stellung	covered position.
Zwischenstellung	intermediate position.
Stellungsbau	field fortification, construction of defences.
Stellungskämpfe ... }	trench warfare.
Stellungskrieg ...	
Stellungswechsel	change of position (*e.g., of a battery*).
Stellvertretend (-er, -e, -es) ...	acting *or* deputy.
Stellvertretender Chef des Generalstabes.	Acting Chief of the General Staff (*in Germany during war*).
Stellvertretendes General-Kommando.	H.Q. of Army Corps District (*in Germany during war*).
Stempel	stamp ; strut, prop.
Stichprobe	inspection ; a test made at random.
Stichwort	code word, pass word.
Stichwörterverzeichnis ...	code.

Stickoxyde	oxides of nitrogen.
Stickstoff	nitrogen.
Stiefelhose	pantaloons.
Stielhandgranate	cylindrical grenade with handle.
Still gestanden !	Attention !
Still sitzen !	Attention ! (*cavalry*).
Stinkraum	gas chamber (*a room for testing gas masks*).
Stirnschutzschild	protection plate for forehead.
Stockung	check, block.
Stockwerksfeuer	tiers of fire.
Stoff	material, cloth.
Stofl (Stabsoffizier der Flieger truppen)	Staff Officer for Aviation (*at Army H.Q.*).
Stollen	deep dug-out ; gallery (*mining, &c., sometimes a main gallery with its branches*).
Abwehrstollen	defensive gallery.
einen Stollen bauen ...	to mine a gallery or dug-out.
flacher Stollen	shallow gallery.
Zweigstollen	branch gallery.
Stollenbaukommando ...	tunnelling party.
Stollenbaukompagnie... ...	tunnelling company.
Stollenbrust	face of a gallery (*mining*).
Stolleneingang	mineshaft, shaft incline.
Stollentreppe	shaft opening.
Stolperdraht	} trip-wire.
Stolperdrahthindernis ...	
Stolperdrahtmine ... , ...	trip-wire mine.
Stoppelfeld	stubble field.
Stoppuhr	stop watch.
Stöpsel	plug (*telephone*).
Stöpselloch	plug-hole (*telephone*).
Störungstrupp	breakdown squad (*telephone, &c.*).
Stoss	attack, raid, thrust ; side wall (*mining*).
Stossbalken	butt plate (*for road bearers of bridge*).
Stossboden	breech block.
Stosssicher	proof against shock.
Strafen	to punish.
eine Strafe aufheben ...	to cancel a punishment.
Straffeuer	retaliation fire.
Straffheit	strictness, strict discipline.
Strandbatterie...	shore battery.
Strassenbaukompagnie ...	road-making company.
Strassenkreuzung	cross roads.

Strassensperre	... ...	barricade.
Strauchwerk ...	... ...	brushwood (*in revetment, &c.*).
Strebe ...	... ...	strut (*mining*).
Streckbalken ...	... ...	road bearers (*bridging*).
Strecke	... ...	stretch, length (*of trench, &c.*), section (*of railway line*) ; gallery (*mining*) ; bay (*of pontoon bridge*).
Streckenarbeiter	... ...	platelayer.
Streckenbau ...	... ...	railway construction.
Streichen	... ...	to extend ; to stroke, graze ; to cancel.
Streifabteilung	... ...	raiding party.
Streifen...	... ...	to graze ; row, band, strip, sector, zone, lane.
Streifkugel	... ...	grazing bullet.
Streifpatrouille	... ...	long distance patrol.
Streifschuss ...	... ...	graze, grazing shot.
Streifzug	... ...	raid.
Streue ...	... ...	litter.
Streuen...	... ...	searching and sweeping fire.
Streukegel	... ...	cone of dispersion.
Streuschiessen	... ...	searching and sweeping fire.
Streuung	... ...	dispersion, irregular shooting, searching and sweeping.
mit geringer Streuung	...	known to shoot accurately.
Seitenstreuung	...	lateral error.
Streuung des Geschützes	...	error in shooting.
Tiefenstreuung	...	error in range, searching.
Streuungsverhältnisse	...	" the 50 per cent. zone."
Strich ...	... ...	stroke, graduation (*on sight, &c.*).
Strichplatte ...	... ...	graticuled field (*optical instruments*).
Strichschiessen	... ...	accurate shooting.
Strickleiter ...	... ...	storming ladder.
Strohkraftfutter	... ...	composite forage.
Strohsack	... ...	paillasse.
Strom ...	... ...	stream ; electric current.
Stromlauf	... ...	circuit (*electric*).
Stube ...	... ...	room, barrack room.
Stück ...	... ...	piece, gun.
Stufe ...	... ...	step.
Stumpfwinklige Trichterladung		overcharged mine (*mining*).
Sturm ...	... ...	assault.
Sturm-Abteilung	...	assault detachment.
Sturmabwehr	...	repelling an assault.
Sturmabwehrgeschütz	...	gun for repelling an assault.
Sturm-Bataillon	... ...	assault battalion.

Sturmgassen	...	passages for the assault (*through wire, &c.*).
Sturmgepäck	...	assault kit.
Sturmkolonne	...	raiding party.
Sturmleiter	...	storming ladder.
Sturmlücke	...	breach.
Sturmmarsch	...	quickened step for assault.
Sturmreifmachen ... Sturmreifschiessen	}	to prepare for the assault, heavy bombardment immediately preceding an assault.
Sturmsignal	...	the " charge."
Sturmstellung	...	position from which an assault is made.
Sturm-Trupp	...	assault detachment.
Sturmvorbereitungsfeuer	...	preparatory bombardment.
Sturm steht bevor ! ...	...	Enemy about to attack !
zum Sturm auf ! ...	...	Charge !
Sturmwelle	...	line *or* wave of assault.
Stute	...	mare.
Stützpunkt	...	strong point.
Stützpunktlinie ...	...	line of strong points.
Subaltern-Offiziere ...	...	subaltern officers.
Summen	...	to buzz.
Summer ... ... Summerapparat ... Summerbrett ...	}	buzzer (*telegraphy*).
Summertaster ...	...	buzzer-key.
Sumpf	...	marsh ; sump (*mining*).
System	...	system ; face (*mining*).

T.

Tagebau	cut and cover construction.
Tagebuch	order book; file of orders.
Tagesanbruch	daybreak.
Tagesbefehl	daily orders.
Tageseinfluss	error of the day (*artillery*).
Tagesrate	ordinary daily allotment (*of gun ammunition*).
Tagewasser	surface water.
Täglicher Dienst	routine.
Tambour	drummer.
Bataillons-Tambour ...	battalion serjeant-drummer.
Tambourmajor	drum-major.
Tankabwehrgeschütz... ...	anti-tank gun.
Tankstelle	petrol depôt.
Taschenmunition	small arms ammunition in pouches.
Taster	key; feeler, antenna.
Tätigkeit	action, activity.
Taube	pigeon; "Taube" (*a make of aeroplane*).
Täuschungsangriff	feint attack.
Täuschungsfeuer Täuschungsschiessen ... }	feint bombardment.
Teile	elements, parties, details.
Teilkartusche	cartridge with adjustable charge (*e.g., howitzer cartridge*).
Teilkreis	graduated circle.
Teilstrich	millième (*field artillery*), or one sixteenth of a degree (*foot artillery*).
Teilstrichzahl	number of graduations.
Telegraphen-Abteilung ...	telegraph detachment.
Telegraphenstange	telegraph post.
Telegraphentruppen	telegraph troops.
Telegraphenwagen	telegraph wagon.
Telephontrupp (des Regiments).	regimental telephone squad.
Tempo (Angriffs-)	pace of the attack.
Teppichhindernis	"Carpet" entanglement.
Termin	time at which a report, &c., should be handed in.
Tiefengliederung	distribution in depth.
Tiefenstreuung	vertical searching fire; error in range.
Tiefenstreuverfahren	searching fire.

Tiefgestaffelt	distributed in depth.
T. Munition	T-shell (*lachrymatory gas shell*).
Titular	brevet.
Tornister	knapsack, pack, valise.
Tracierband	tracing tape.
Tragbalken	transom (*bridging*) ; beam.
Tragbar	portable.
Trage	stretcher.
Tragegurt	belt (*for carrying an infantry shield, &c.*).
Trageknüppel	support.
Träger	carrier, bearer ; girder.
Trägerkommando ...	} carrying party.
Trägertrupp	
Tragetier	pack animal.
Tragweite	range.
Tränenerregend	lachrymatory.
Tränenreiz	irritation of the eyes (*caused by lachrymatory shells*).
Train	Train (*not translated*).
Traindepot	Train depôt.
Trainfahrer	driver of the Train.
Trainsoldat	private of the Train.
Tränke	watering place for horses.
Tränken ... ... · ...	to water (*horses, &c.*).
Transportfähig	fit for transport, able to be evacuated (*wounded*).
Transportkommando ...	details to accompany wounded or prisoners.
Trasse	trace (*e.g., of a new trench*).
Treibkraft	propelling power.
Treibladung	propelling charge.
Treibmaschine...	propeller.
Treffenweise	units one in rear of the other.
Treffer	direct hit.
Trefferbild	plotting of the fall of shots.
Trefffähigkeit	} accuracy of fire.
Treffgenauigkeit ...	
Treffpunkt	point of impact.
Treffsicherheit	accuracy of fire.
Tresse	braid.
Treten	to tread.
Tretmine	contact mine (*actuated by treading on it*).
Trichter	mine crater, shell hole.
Trichterfeld	crater area.
Trichterladung (Stumpfwinklige).	overcharged mine (*mining*).

Trichterwirkung	crater effect.
Trigonometrisch	trigonometrical, by triangulation.
Trigonometrischer Punkt	trigonometrical point.
Tritt	step.
Trommelfeuer	intense *or* heavy bombardment.
Trompeter	trumpeter.
Tross	baggage, impedimenta of an army.
Trosswagen	baggage wagon.
Trümmer	ruins, débris.
Trupp	section, party, squad.
Truppe	regimental officers and men (*as compared with the staff*).
Truppen	troops.
Truppenbewegungen	troops on the move.
Truppeneinteilung	distribution of troops, order of battle.
Truppenführer	commander.
Truppenkette	cordon.
Truppensammlung	concentration of troops.
Truppenteil	unit.
Truppenübungsplatz	training ground.
Truppenverband	formation.
Truppenverbandplatz	regimental aid post.
Truppenverpflegung	provisioning of troops.
Truppenverschiebungen	changes in the disposition of troops.
Truppenvorgesetzte	unit commanders, commanding officers.
Tschako	shako.
Tschapka	lancer cap.
T-Träger	T-girder.
Tuch	cloth, linen; cloth signal.
Tuchzeichen	linen signal.
Turm	tower, turret.
Turmhaubitze	howitzer in turret.
Turmkanone	gun in turret.
Turmlafette	turret mounting.
Turnübung	gymnastic exercise.
Tusche	Indian (Chinese) ink.
Typhus	typhoid (*not typhus*).

U.

Überbank feuern	to fire over the parapet.
Überbleibsel	remainder.
Überbringen	to convey.
einen Befehl überbringen ...	to deliver an order.
Überbringer	carrier, bearer.
Überdeckung	cover.
Übereinstimmung (bringen in)	to synchronize (watches); agreement, accord, unanimity.
Überfall	raid, surprise attack.
Übergabe	surrender, giving up.
Übergang	crossing, passage (of a river).
Übergangsstadium	state of transition.
Übergangsstation	transfer station (on L. of C.).
Übergehen	to change over to (artillery fire).
Überläufer	deserter.
Überlegenheit ... ... ⎫	
Übermacht ... ... ⎭	superiority.
Übernehmen	to take over (e.g., a position).
das Kommando übernehmen	to take command of.
die Verantwortung übernehmen.	to assume responsibility for.
Überrumpeln	to surprise.
Überrumpelung	" coup de main."
Überschauen	to overlook, survey.
Überschreiten	to cross, pass.
Überschrift	heading.
Überschwemmung	inundation.
Übersehen	to overlook, dominate.
Übersicht	survey, view.
Übersichtlich	clear.
Übersichtskarte	outline map.
Übersichtsskizze	general sketch of the neighbourhood.
Überspringen	to pass beyond.
Übersteigen	to surmount, cross, exceed.
Überstreichen	to pass over (of a gas cloud).
Übertragen	to entrust, transfer.
Übertreten	to come under (the order of).
Übertretung	contravention, infringement, violation.
Überweisung	allotment, transfer.
Überwiegend	predominating.
Überzug	cover (of helmet, &c.).
Übung	training, practice, exercise.
Übungsgranate	practice shell.

Übungshandgranate	dummy hand grenade.
Übungsladung...	practice charge.
Übungsmaske	practice mask (*gas*).
Übungsmunition	practice ammunition.
Übungsplatz	training ground.
Uferbalken	shore transom (*bridging*).
Ulan	Ulan (*lancer*).
Ulanen-Regiment	" Ulanen " regiment (*lancer regiment*).
Ulanka	lancer tunic.
Umbau (in)	in course of reconstruction.
Umbetten	to " slew " (*e.g., a trench mortar*).
Umdruck	copies for distribution (*orders, &c.*).
Umfassen	to outflank.
Umfassungsbewegung ...	outflanking movement.
Umfüllpumpe	compression pump.
Umgang	breeching (*harness*).
Umgeändert ... ... ⎫	
Umgearbeitet ... ... ⎬ converted.
Umgehängt	slung.
Umgehen	to turn (*a position*), envelop.
Umgehend	by return.
Umgehungsbewegung... ...	turning movement.
Umhang	cape.
Umlagerung	removal (*of ammunition, &c.*).
Umlauf, in	to be circulated (*often found at foot of orders*).
Umlaufmotor	rotary engine.
Umquartieren...	to change quarters.
Umschnallen	to put on (*equipment*).
Umsicht	caution, discretion, wariness.
Umstand	circumstance.
Umstehend	as stated overleaf.
Umtausch	turnover (*of stores*).
Unausgebildet	untrained.
Ungezieltes Feuer	unaimed fire.
Uniform	uniform.
Uniform, dunkelblaue ...	" dark blue " uniform. (*as opposed to " field service "*).
Uniform, feldgraue	field-grey field service uniform.
Uniform, graugrüne	grey-green field service uniform.
Uniformstücke	articles of uniform.
Unklare Elemente	suspects.
Unschädlich machen	to put out of action.
Untauglich	unfit.
dauernd untauglich ...	permanently unfit.
Unterabschnitt	sub-sector.
Unterabschnittskommandeur	sub-sector commander.

Unterarzt	sub-surgeon (*warrant officer*).
Unterbleiben	to remain undone.
Unterbringen	to billet, accommodate, station.
Unterbringung	billeting ; storage (*of ammunition,* &c.).
Unterführer	subordinate commander.
Untergebener	subordinate.
Untergestellen	pivots.
Untergurt	girth.
Unterhalten	to entertain ; to sustain, maintain.
ein heftiges Feuer unterhalten.	to keep up a heavy fire.
Unterkommandeur	subordinate commander.
Unterkunft	billet.
Unterkunftslager	rest camp.
Unterlage(n)	basis, data.
Unterlassen	cancelling (*of an attack*).
Unterliegen	to succumb, suffer defeat.
Unternehmen	to undertake.
Unternehmen ... ... ⎱	enterprise, operation.
Unternehmung ... ... ⎰	
Unteroffizier	non-commissioned officer ; *also* " under-officer " *which is a special rank of N.C.O. corresponding to our corporal.*
Unterricht	instruction.
Unterrichts-	instructional.
Unterschlupf	shelter, " funk hole," recess.
Unterschrieben	signed.
Unterschrift	signature.
Unterstand	dug-out, shelter.
Unterstandstreppe	steps leading down to a dug-out.
Unterstehen	to be subordinate to.
Unterstellen	to place under the orders of.
Unterstützen	to support.
Unterstützung...	support, assistance.
Unterstützungsgraben ...	support trench.
zur Unterstützung der Posten	to reinforce the sentries.
Unterstützungstruppen ...	reinforcements.
Untersuchen	to inquire, examine, test, inspect.
Untertreteraum	dug-out.
Unterveterinär	sub-veterinary surgeon (*warrant officer*).
Unterwasserschneide-Abteilung.	divers detachment.
Urlaub	leave.
Urlauber	man on leave.

Urlaubsschein ...	...	...	pass *or* furlough.
Urlaubszug	...	...	... leave train.
Urschrift	...	...	... original document.

V.

Vedette	vedette.
Ventil	valve.
Verankerung	holding down ; anchorage.
Veranlagung (körperliche) ...	physique.
Verantwortung	responsibility.
Verästelung	shower (*of sparks from rocket*).
Verband	formation.
Verbandabteilung	surgical dressing detachment (*of main dressing station*).
Verbandpäckchen	first field dressing.
Verbandplatz ... ... ⎫	
Verbandraum ... ... ⎬	dressing station, first-aid post.
Verbandstelle ... ... ⎭	
Verbandzeug	surgical bandage.
Verbandzeugtornister ...	bandage case.
Verbindung	communication, connection, liaison.
Verbindungsbahn	junction railway.
Verbindungsgalerie	transversal gallery (*mining*).
Verbindungsgraben	communication trench.
Verbindungs-Offizier	liaison officer.
Verbindungsstollen ... ... ⎫	transversal gallery (*mining*).
Verbindungsstrecke ... ... ⎭	
Verbolzen	to bolt together.
Verbrauch	consumption, expenditure (*e.g., of ammunition*).
Verbringen	to dispose of.
Verbündeten (die)	the Allies.
Verdämmen	to tamp (*mining*).
Verdecken	to mask (*fire*).
Verdienstorden	Order of Merit.
Vereinbarung	co-operation, arrangement, agreement.
Vereinslazarett	auxiliary hospital.
Verfahren	procedure, method, system, action.
Verfeuern	to fire off.
Verfolgen	to pursue.
Verfügbar	available.
Verfügen über	to have at one's disposal.
Verfügungen	instructions.
zur Verfügung	available.
zur Verfügung stellen ...	to place at disposal.
Vergeltungsfeuer	retaliatory fire.
Vergossen	grouted (*with cement*).
Verhalten	behaviour, action, procedure.
Verhältnis	circumstance, proportion, relation.

Verhau	abatis.
Verheeren	to ravage, devastate.
Verhör	cross-examination.
Verhören	to examine (*prisoners*).
Verkehr	traffic.
Verkehrsgraben	supervision *or* lateral communication trench.
Verkehrsmittel	means of transport.
Verkehrsoffizier vom Platz ...	fortress communication officer.
Verkehrstruppen	communication troops.
Verkehrswesen	communication service.
Verkleiden	to disguise, mask, to revet.
Verkleidung	revetment.
Verläufer	straggler.
Verlautbaren	to proclaim.
Verlegen	to transfer.
Feuer rückwärts verlegen ...	to shorten range.
Feuer vorwärts verlegen ...	to lengthen range.
Verlegung	relaying (*of a telephone circuit*).
Verletzung	injury.
Verletzungsliste	casualty list.
Verluste	losses, casualties.
Verlustliste	casualty list.
Vermessung	survey.
Vermessungs-Abteilung ...	survey section.
Vermisste	missing, stragglers.
Vermittlung	telephone exchange ; intervention.
Vermorel-Apparat	Vermorel sprayer.
Vernehmung	examination (*e.g., of prisoners*).
Vernichtung	annihilation, destruction.
Vernichtungsfeuer	annihilating fire.
Vernickelt	nickel-plated.
Verordnungsblatt (Armee-)	Army Orders.
Verpassen	to test, to adjust (*e.g., a gas mask*).
Verpassungsraum	gas testing chamber.
Verpflegung	supply (*food*), rationing.
Vorbringen der Verpflegung	carrying up rations.
Konserven-Verpflegung ...	tinned rations.
Verpflegungsabteilung ...	supply section of the Intendance.
Verpflegungsgebühr ...	scale of rations.
Verpflegungskolonne ...	supply column.
Verpflegungsmittel	rations.
Verpflegungsnachschub ...	supply of rations, bringing up rations.
Verpflegungs-Offizier ...	supply officer.
Verpflegungsstärke ...	ration strength.
Verpflegungstruppen ...	supply troops.

Verpflegungszug	supply train (*railway*).
Verraten (eine Stellung) ...	to disclose (a position); to betray.
Verriegelung	barricade of timber used in tamping (*mining*).
Versagen	to miss fire; to break down.
Versager	a misfire, "blind" (*shell*).
Versammlungsgraben... ...	assembly trench.
Verschalung	revetting.
Verschalbretter	boards for revetting.
Verschanzung	entrenchment.
Verschanzung aufwerfen ...	to throw up an entrenchment.
Verschieben	to move (*troops, &c.*).
Verschiessen	to fire away, expend.
Verschleierung	masking, concealment.
Verschluss	breech (*of gun or rifle*).
Verschlussteile	breech fittings.
Verschlusskappe	cap of fuze.
Verschütten	bury alive; to block up (*e.g., with earth*).
Gräben werden leicht ver- schüttet.	trenches soon fall in.
Verschütterung	collapse (*of a dug-out*).
Verschüttet.	buried.
Versetzung	transfer.
Verspreizung	strutting (*mining, &c.*).
Versprengter	straggler.
Verständigung...	hearing signals (*on telephone, &c.*).
Ist Verständigung gut ? ...	Are signals good ? (*on telephone, &c.*).
Verstärken	to strengthen, reinforce.
Verstärkung	reinforcement.
Versteifern	to strut (*mining, &c.*).
Verstreben	to brace (*e.g., the frames of a dug- out*).
Versuch	experiment, trial, test.
Versuchsanstalt	experimental laboratory *or* institute.
Verteidigen	to defend.
Verteidigungsanlagen... ...	defences, defence works.
Verteidigungsfähig	capable of defence.
Verteidigungsstellung ...	defensive position.
Verteilung	distribution.
Verteilungstafel	switchboard (*on to which the leads for testing and firing mines are brought*).
Vertretung (in)	"By order," "Signed for" (*above a signature on a document*).
Vervielfältigen	to reproduce (*e.g., by printing, hectograph, &c.*).

Verwaltung	administration.	
Armeeverwaltungs-Departe-ment	Army Administrative Department.	
Feldverwaltungs-Behörden	field administrative authorities.	
Verwaltungsbeamte	administrative official.	
Verwaltungsbehörden ...	administrative authorities.	
Verweis	reprimand.	
Verwenden	to use, employ, make use of.	
Verzeichnis	list.	
Verzögerung	delay, delay action.	
Veterinär	Second-lieutenant	
Generalveterinär	Colonel.	
Korpsstabsveterinär ...	Major.	(veterinary).
Oberstabsveterinär ...	brevet Major.	
Stabsveterinär	Captain.	
Oberveterinär	Lieutenant.	
Vieleck	polygon.	
Viereck	quadrangle, square, rectangle.	
Vierkantholz	squared timber.	
Vierzöllig	4-inch.	
Visier	sight (of rifle), especially back sight.	
Visieraufsatzstange	leaf of back sight.	
Visierfernrohr	dial sight.	
Vizefeldwebel	vice-serjeant-major.	
Vizewachtmeister	vice-serjeant-major (mounted troops).	
Vollbahn	standard gauge railway.	
Vollkriegsfähig	fit for active service.	
Vollsalve	complete salvo.	
Vollspurbahn	standard gauge railway.	
Vollstrecken	to carry out (a punishment).	
Volltreffer	direct hit.	
Vollzug	execution of orders.	
Vollzugsmeldung	report of execution of orders.	
Vorbereitung	preparation.	
Vorbereitungsfeuer	preparatory bombardment.	
Vorbohrer	rimer.	
Vorderbracke	swingle-tree.	
Vorbringen (der Verpflegung)	carrying up (rations).	
Vorderkaffe	bow (of a pontoon).	
Vorderlader	muzzle loader.	
Vordermann	front rank man.	
Vorderpferd	lead horse.	
Vorderwagen	limber.	
Vordringen	to advance.	
Vorführen	to bring up, lead forward.	
Vorgehen	to advance.	

Vorgelände	foreground, " No man's land."
Vorgesetzter	superior.
Vorhanden	existing, available.
Vorholfedern	running out springs (gun).
Vorhut	advanced guard.
Vorlage...	proposal; text.
Vorlegen (Feuer)	to lengthen range.
Vornewand	face (of a mine).
Vorposten	outposts.
Vorposten ausstellen	to throw out outposts.
Vorpostengefecht	affair of outposts.
Vorpostenkette	chain of sentries.
Vorpostenkommandeur ...	outpost commander.
Vorpostenkompagnie ...	outpost company.
Vorpostenlinie...	outpost line.
Vorratspferd	spare horse.
Vorratswagen	store wagon.
Vorraum (eines Unterstandes)	anteroom (to a dug-out).
Vorrichtung	device, arrangement, mechanism.
Vorschieben	to push forward, advance.
Vorschrift	regulations.
Vorstecker	safety pin (of fuze).
Vorstoss	attack, raid, thrust ; piping, edging (uniform).
Vortrab	vanguard.
Vortreiben	to run out, drive (a gallery) (mining, &c.).
Vortrupp	vanguard.
Vortruppen	advanced troops.
Vorverlegen	to " lift " (artillery fire).
Vorwärts	forward.
Vorwerk	advanced work ; farm ; manor (" Vw." on a military map).
Vorziehen	to move up ; to give preference to.

W.

Wache ...	guard, sentry.
Wachhabender	officer (n.c.o.) of the guard.
Wachposten ...	sentry.
Wachstuchmütze	waterproof cap (*worn by Landwehr*).
Wachtdienst ...	guard duty.
Wachthabender	officer (n.c.o.) of the guard.
Wachtmeister ...	serjeant-major (*of cavalry or field artillery*).
Wachtturm ...	watch tower (*topog*).
Waffe ...	weapon, arm.
Waffengattung	arm of the service.
Waffenhaus ...	arsenal.
Waffenmeister	armourer ; artificer.
Waffenmeisterkasten	artificer's tool chest.
Waffenmittelwagen ...	travelling repair shop.
Waffenrock ...	tunic.
Waffenruhe ... ⎱ Waffenstillstand ⎰	armistice.
Wagenburg ...	barricade of wagons.
Wagenfähre ...	ferry for wagons.
Wagengerassel...	the rattling of carts or wagons.
Wagenhalteplatz ...	halting place for ambulance vehicles.
Wagenstaffel ...	wagon line.
Wagerecht ...	horizontal.
Wahrnehmung	observation.
Waldstück ...	small wood.
Wall ...	rampart.
Wallgraben ...	moat, ditch of rampart.
Wallmeister ...	staff serjeant of fortifications
Walzblech ...	rolled iron plate.
Walzblei ...	sheet lead.
Walze (Draht-) ...	roller, cylinder (*e.g., of wire*).
Walzeisen ...	rolled iron.
Walzen ...	to roll, roll out.
Wand ...	wall.
Wappen ...	armorial bearings.
Wassereimer ...	water bucket.
Wassergraben ...	drainage channel (*mining, &c.*).
Wasserkasten ...	water jacket.
Wasserleitung ...	water supply, aqueduct.
Wasserleitungsröhre ...	water pipe, conduit pipe.
Wässern ...	to irrigate.
Wasserschaufel ...	water scoop (*pontoon*).

Wasserstoff	...	...	hydrogen.
Wassertragesack	...	...	canvas water bucket.
Wasserversorgung	...	...	supply of water, water supply.
Wasserwage ...	...	...	water-level.
Wasserzapfstelle	...	...	water tank.
Wechselgetrieb	...	...	variable gear.
Wechselstellung	...	...	alternative emplacement.
Wechselstrom ...	...	...	alternating current (electrical).
Weckerapparat	...	...	magneto-ringing apparatus (telephone).
Weg	...	...	road, way, track.
Wegekarte	...	...	route map.
Wegekreuz ...	...	...	} road junction, cross roads.
Wegekreuzung	...	...	
Wegverlegen ...	...	...	to " lift " (artillery fire).
Wegweiser	...	...	finger post, signboard.
Wehrordnung ...	...	...	regulations dealing with conscription laws.
Wehrpflicht ...	...	...	liability for service.
Weiche ...	...	...	points (railway).
Weichen ...	...	...	to yield, give way, give ground.
Weissblech ...	...	...	tin plate.
Weisungen ...	...	...	instructions.
Weit	...	...	" over " (artillery).
Weiterleitung ...	...	...	circulation (of orders).
Weiterleitungsstelle ...	...	...	forwarding office (e.g., of Army Clothing Depôt).
Wellblech ...	...	...	corrugated iron.
Wellblechdecke	...	...	corrugated iron cover.
Wellblechfelder	...	...	corrugated iron sheets.
Wellblechrahmen	...	...	corrugated iron section.
Wellblechschalung	...	...	corrugated iron lining.
Welle	...	...	wave.
Wellenlänge ...	...	...	wave length (wireless, &c.).
Wendeplatz ...	...	...	turntable, place for turning vehicles.
Wendepunkt ...	...	...	critical moment, turning point.
Wendesappe ...	...	...	wavy sap.
Wendung ...	...	...	turn.
Werfer	...	...	" thrower " (bomber).
Werfer ...	...	...	sometimes used for " Minenwerfer."
Werferführer ...	...	...	N.C.O. in charge of trench mortar.
Werferstand ...	...	...	trench mortar emplacement.
Werk	...	...	work, redoubt.
Werkstatt	...	...	workshop.
Werkstelle			
Werkzeugkasten	...	...	tool chest.

Werkzeugtasche	... ...	tool wallet.
Werkzeugwagen	... ...	tool wagon.
Wetterbeobachtung	... ...	meteorological observation.
'Wetterbericht	... ...	meteorological report.
Wetterdienst ...	... ...	meteorological service.
Wetterlage	... ...	weather conditions.
Wetterlotte ...	... ...	air pipe (*mining*).
Wickelgamasche	... ...	puttee.
Widerstand ...	... ...	resistance ; electrical resistance.
Widerstandsfähig	... ...	capable of resistance.
Widerstandskraft } Widerstandsvermögen	...	defensive power, resisting power.
Widerstreben ...	... ...	to oppose, resist.
Wiederherstellen	... ...	to repair.
Wiege	... ...	cradle of a gun.
Windewagen ...	... ...	windlass wagon (*balloon detachment*).
Windfächer ...	... ...	fan.
Windfähnchen...	... ...	weather cock.
Windfahne ...	... ...	anemoscope (*flag*).
Windrosendarstellung	...	wind-compass card.
Windsbraut ...	... ...	gust of wind, squall.
Windstärkemesser	... ...	anemometer.
Windstoss ...	... ...	gust of wind.
Winkel	...	angle.
ausspringender Winkel	...	salient.
einspringender Winkel	...	re-entrant.
toter Winkel ...	...	dead ground.
vorspringender Winkel } vorstehender Winkel	...	salient.
Winkeleisen ...	... ...	angle iron.
Winkelfernrohr	... ...	periscope.
Winkelmesser ...	... ...	clinometer, goniometer.
Winkertrupp ...	... ...	flag signalling group (*all arms*).
Winkerverbindung	... ...	flag signalling communication.
Winkerzeichen	... ...	flag signals.
Wirksamkeit ...	... ...	efficacy.
Wirkung ...	... ...	effect.
Wirkungsbereich	... ...	effective range, sphere of operations.
Wirkungshalbmesser ...	...	radius of explosion (*mining*).
Wirkungsschiessen ...	...	effective bombardment, fire for effect.
Wirtschaftskompagnie	...	tradesman company.
Wischen	...	to wipe.
Wischer	...	pull-through ; sponge.
Wischfalte	...	cleaning fold (*of German gas mask*).
Wohngraben ...	... ...	living trench.
Wohnunterstand	... ...	living dug-out.

Woilach	saddle blanket.
Wolfsgrube	" trou de loup."
Wumba. (Waffen und Munitions-Beschaffungs-Amt).	Munitions Department of the War Ministry.
Wurfgeschwindigkeit ...	rate of fire.
Wurfgranate	trench mortar bomb.
Wurfladung·	propelling charge.
Wurfladung (Ladungsmine) ...	canister bomb.
Wurflinie	trajectory.
Wurfmine	mine, *Minenwerfer* shell (*the modern term is* " *Sprengmine*," *q.v.*)
lange schwere (l.s.W.M.) ...	25 cm. heavy *Minenwerfer* (long H.E. shell).
kurze schwere (k.s.W.M.) ...	25 cm. heavy *Minenwerfer* (short H.E. shell).
mittlere gezogene (m.gez. W.M.).	17 cm. medium rifled *Minenwerfer* (H.E. shell).
mittlere glatte (m.gl.W.M.)	(?) 17 cm. medium smooth bore *Minenwerfer* (H.E. shell).
leichte gezogene (l.gez.W.M.)	7.5 cm. light rifled *Minenwerfer* (H.E. shell).
glatte leichte (Lanz) (gl.l. W.M. Lanz).	9.1 cm. light smooth bore Lanz *Minenwerfer* (H.E. shell).
Wurfweite	length of throw.

Z.

Zähigkeit	... ...	tenacity, obstinacy.
Zahl und Art ...	... ...	quantity and nature.
Zahlmeister	... ...	paymaster.
Zahnrad	... ...	cogged wheel.
Zange ...	... ...	pincers, tongs.
Zapfen ...	... ...	trunnions (of gun), pin, plug, pivot.
Zapfenlager	... ...	trunnion bed (of gun).
Zapfenstreich ...	... ...	tattoo, " retreat."
Zaum ...	... ...	bridle.
Zaumzeug	... ...	headgear.
Zaun ...	... ...	fence.
Zeche ...	... ...	pit, mine, coalshaft.
Zeichen...	... ...	sign, signal, distinguishing mark.
Zeichner	... ...	draughtsman.
Zeigefinger	... ...	index finger.
Zeiger ...	... ...	index, indicator ; hand of a clock.
Zeitangabe	... ...	date.
Zeiteinteilung ...	... ...	time table.
Zeitschnur	... ...	safety fuze.
Zeitweilig	... ...	intermittent.
Zelt ...	... ...	tent.
Zelt aufschlagen	... ...	to pitch a tent.
Zeltbahn	... ...	tent square.
Zeltpflock	... ...	tent peg.
Zeltstange	... ...	tent pole.
Zementmörtel	... ...	cement mortar.
Zementsack ...	... ...	cement sack.
Zentner	... ...	½ quintal = 50 kg. = 110.23 lbs.
Zentralnachweisebureau	...	Central Information Bureau.
Zentrierwulst ...	... ...	shoulder of a shell.
Zermürben	... ...	to crush.
Zernierung	... ...	blockade.
Zersplittern	... ...	to splinter, break to pieces ; to disperse (e.g., troops, fire, &c.).
Zersprengen	... ...	to cut up, rout.
Zerstören	... ...	destroy, demolish, cut (wire entanglement).
Zerstörung	... ...	demolition.
Zerstörungsfeuer	... ...	destructive fire .
Zerstreuen	... ...	to scatter.
Zertrümmern ...	... ...	to wreck, break in pieces.
Zeug ...	... ...	prefixed to rank = ordnance.
Zeug ...	... ...	material.
Zeugamt	... ...	Ordnance Department.

Zeugdepot	...	ordnance depôt.
Zeuge ...	...	witness.
Zeughaus	...	arsenal, armoury.
Zeugoffizier	...	ordnance officer.
Zeugpersonal ...	...	ordnance corps.
Ziegelei	...	brick-field, tile works.
Ziegelstein	...	brick.
Ziehen ...	...	to draw, move.
Ziehen (auseinander) ...	...	to keep extended.
Ziel ...	...	objective ; target, aim.
Zielabschnitt ...	...	target sector, sector to be taken under fire.
Zielbezeichnung	...	designation of targets.
Zielen ...	...	to aim.
Zielerkundung	...	reconnaissance of a target.
Zielfernrohr ...	...	telescopic sight.
Zielpunkt	...	objective ; point aimed at.
Zielscheibe	...	target.
Zielskizze	...	range card.
Zielspiegel	...	periscope.
Zielstation	...	destination ; railhead.
Zielstreifen	...	target sector.
Zieltafeln	...	target tables.
Zielwechsel	...	change of target.
Zielzuweisung ...	...	indication of targets.
Zierat ...	...	ornaments (on helmet, &c.).
Ziffer (Ziff.) ...	...	paragraph ; cipher ; numeral.
Zimmermann ...	...	carpenter.
Zinnfolie	...	tinfoil.
Zivilbevölkerung	...	civil population.
Zivilkleidung (or Zivil)	...	plain clothes.
Zollbeamte	...	customs official.
Zone ...	...	sector, zone, area.
Zubehör	...	accessories.
Zubehörkasten	...	box containing accessories.
Zubereiten	...	to prepare (food).
Zubereiter	...	fitter.
Zucht ...	...	discipline ; breeding (horses, cattle).
Züchten	...	to breed.
Zufahrtsweg ...	...	track leading up to a position, approach.
Zufallstreffer ...	...	chance hit.
Zuflucht	...	refuge, shelter ; recourse.
Zufuhr ...	...	the bringing up of supplies.
Zufuhr abschneiden ...	...	to cut off supplies.
Zufuhrstrasse	...	approach.
Zu Fuss (Garde-Regiment) ...	Foot (Guards).

Zug	platoon, section, cavalry troop (*of* 3 *or more* "*Groups*"); train; rifling (*of a gun*).
Zugang	admission to hospital, &c.; access, approach.
Zugangsgraben ... ⎫	communication trench, approach
Zugangsweg ... ... ⎬	trench.
Zugbrücke	drawbridge.
Zügel	rein, bridle.
Zugeteilt	attached to, allotted to.
Zugführer	platoon (section) commander.
Zugkolonne	column of platoons.
Zugloch	ventilator.
Zugpferd	draught horse.
Zugsbereich	platoon sector.
Zugtau	drag rope.
Zugweise	by platoons.
Zulage	extra pay; allowance.
Zulegen	to add to.
50 Meter zulegen!	Plus 50 metres! Lengthen range 50 metres!
Zündbolzen	percussion pellet (*fuze*).
Zünder	fuze, detonator.
Aufschlagzünder	percussion fuze.
Brennzünder	time fuze.
Doppelzünder	time and percussion fuze.
Innenzünder	internal fuze.
Kopfzünder	nose fuze.
Kurzer Bodenzünder ...	short base fuze.
Langer Bodenzünder ...	long base fuze.
Zünderschlüssel	fuze key.
Zünder stellen...	to set a fuze.
Zünderstellmaschine	fuze setter.
Zünderteller	ring of a fuze.
Zündfertig	ready for firing.
Zündglocke (Amboss der) ...	detonator cap.
Zündhütchen	percussion cap.
Zündkapsel	detonator.
Zündkasten	exploder (*mining*).
Zündladung	exploder (*in a shell*).
Zündloch	vent.
Zündmittel	means of ignition (*fuzes, detonators, &c.*).
Zündröhre	fuze, friction tube.
Zündsatz	detonating composition.
Zündschnur	fuze, safety fuze; lanyard.
Zündung	fuze, primer *and* detonator; *also* the firing of a charge.

Zur Disposition (z. D.)	on half pay (*of officers*).
Zureicher	carrier *in a bombing squad, the man who hands the grenade to the thrower.*
Zuruf	call, verbal message.
Zusammenarbeiten	to co-operate, co-operation.
Zusammenfassen	to concentrate.
Zusammensetzen (Gewehr)	to pile (arms).
Zusammensetzung	composition.
Zusammenstoss	collision.
Zusammentreffen	to meet, encounter.
Zusammentreten	to stand to.
Zusammentritt	assembly, parade.
Zusammenwirken	co-operation, to co-operate.
Zusammenziehen (Truppen)	to assemble, concentrate.
Zusatz	supplement.
Zuschuss	allowance.
Zusprechen	to adjudge, agree with.
Zuständiger Arzt	medical officer on duty.
Zustellen	to transmit, deliver, convey.
Zurückgehen	to retreat, retire, fall back.
Zurückhaltung	reticence, reserve.
Zurücklaufen	to recoil (*gun*).
Zurückschlagen	to beat off, repulse.
Zurückweichen	to recoil, fall back.
Zuteilen	to attach; to allot to.
Zuteilung	allotment ; attachment.
Zuverlässig	reliable.
Zuweisung	allotment.
Zuwiderhandlung	infringement, violation, contravention.
Zweck	objective, purpose, object.
Zweidecker	biplane.
Zweigstollen	branch gallery (*mining*).
Zwickzange	tweezers.
Zwieback	biscuit.
Zwischendepot	intermediate dump or depôt.
Zwischengelände	intervening country.
Zwischenpark	intermediate park.
Zwischenpolster	intermediate cushion (*e.g., of earth over a dug-out*).
Zwischenraum	interval.
in Zwischenräumen	intermittently (*artillery fire*).
Zwischenstellung	intermediate position.
Zwischenzeit	meantime.
Zwischenzeiten	pauses.
mit Zwischenzeiten	intermittently (*artillery fire*).

ABBREVIATIONS.

Method of using Abbreviations in Orders.

In the German Field Service Regulations, 1908, paragraph 105, the following examples are given of the employment of abbreviations in orders, reports, &c. :—

I. R. 130	130th Infantry Regiment.
St. I. u. II/27, *or* I.R. 27 St. I. II. ...	Staff, and 1st and 2nd Battalions, 27th Infantry Regiment ; *or* 27th Infantry Regiment, Staff, 1st and 2nd Battalions.
I.R. 67 (ohne 11.)	67th Infantry Regiment (less the 11th Company).
Jäg. 3	3rd *Jäger* Battalion.
M.G.A. 1	Machine Gun Detachment No. 1.
St. 1. 3. 4./Ul 14 *or* Ul. 14 (ohne 2.)...	Staff, 1st 3rd and 4th Squadrons, 14th *Ulanen* Regt. ; *or* 14th *Ulanen* Regt. (less the 2nd Squadron).
St. u. R/F. A. 34 *or* F.A. 34 St. u. R.	Staff and Horse Artillery *Abteilung*, 34th Field Artillery Regiment; *or* 34th Field Artillery Regiment, Staff and Horse Artillery *Abteilung*.
II (F) F.A. 4	2nd *Abteilung* (field howitzer) of Field Artillery Regiment 4.
St. u. I (s. F.H.)/Fuss-A. 4	Staff and 1st (heavy field howitzer) Battalion of 4th Foot Artillery Regiment.
II (Mrs.)/Fuss-A.5	2nd Battalion (mortar) of 5th Foot Artillery Regiment
1./Pi. 3	1st Company, 3rd Pioneer Battalion.
S.K. 2	2nd Bearer Company.
K. Tel. A.	Corps Telegraph Detachment.

ABBREVIATIONS.

Abbreviation.	Signification.	English Equivalent.
	A	
A....	Art	pattern.
A....	Abteilung	" Abteilung " (*sometimes* "*detachment*").
A.A.	Armee-Abteilung ...	Army Detachment (*equivalent to an Army*).
a/A.	alter Art	old pattern.
A. Abt	Artillerie-Abteilung ...	artillery " Abteilung."
a. B.	auf Befehl	" By order," " Signed for " (*above a signature in a document*).

Abbreviation.	Signification.	English Equivalent.
Abt. ⎫ Abtlg. ⎬ ... ... Abtl. ⎭	Abteilung	section, detachment, flight, &c.; "Abteilung" (*not translated in the case of field artillery, when it is a group of 3 batteries*).
A.B. zur Fp.D.O.	Ausführungs-Bestimmungen zur Feldpost Dienstordnung	Instructions for the Execution of the Regulations for the Field Post.
a.D.	ausser Dienst	retired (*of officers*).
A.E.G.	Allgemeine-Elektricitäts-Gesellschaft.	(*A firm which manufactures aeroplanes, fuzes and other war material*).
Afla.	Artillerie-Flieger-Abteilung ...	artillery flight.
A. Gr.	Artillerie-Gruppe	artillery group.
Agru ...	Arendt-Gruppe	listening set section.
A.H.Kw. ...	Armee-Hauptkwartier ...	Army Headquarters.
A.H.Q. ⎫ A.HQu. ⎭ ...	Armee-Hauptquartier... ...	Army Headquarters.
A.K.	Armee-Korps	Army Corps, Corps.
A.K.O.	Allerhöchste-Kabinetts-Ordre	Order of His Majesty in Council.
Akofern.	Armee-Fernsprech-Kommando.	Army Telephone H.Q.
A.m.F.b. ...	... ...	(*before a signature*).
Akofunk ...	Armee-Funker-Kommando ...	Army Wireless H.Q.
A.M.K.	Artillerie-Munitions-Kolonne	artillery ammunition column.
an.	angekommen	arrived.
A.O.K.	Armee-Oberkommando ...	Army Headquarters (*Staff*).
Arm. Batl. ...	Armierungs-Bataillon ...	labour battalion.
Ara	Arendt-Abteilung	listening set detachment.
Art. ⎫ Artl. ⎭	Artillerie	artillery.
A.S.	Acetylen-Sauerstoff	oxyacetylene (*used in portable searchlight and signalling lamps*).
Asto	Arendt-Station	listening set.
A.T.-Station ...	... ...	power buzzer station.
A.T.B. ...	Armee-Tages-Befehl	Army Daily Order.
Aufgeb.	Aufgebot	ban (*of Landsturm or Landwehr*).
Av.	Arbeitsverwendungsfähig ...	suitable for employment for labour.
A.V.B.	Armee-Verordnungs-Blatt ...	Army Orders.
A.V.F.	Arbeitsverwendungsfähig im Felde.	fit for labour employment in the field.
A.V.G.	Arbeitsverwendungsfähig in der Garnison.	fit for labour employment in Germany.
A.V.O.	Artillerie-Verbindungs-Offizier	artillery liaison officer.
Az.	Aufschlag-Zünder	percussion fuze.

Abbreviation.	Signification.	English Equivalent.

B.

B.	Bach	stream, brook (*topog.*).
B.	Bataillon	battalion.
B. ... ` ...	Berg	mountain (*topog.*).
b.	bayerisch	Bavarian.
B.A.	Bekleidungsamt	clothing office *or* depôt.
Bäck. Kol. ...	(Feld-)Bäckerei-Kolonne ...	(field) bakery column.
B.A.K.Z.... ...	Ballon-Abwehr-Kanonen-Zug	anti-aircraft section.
Batl.	Bataillon	battalion.
Bat. ⎫ ⎬ ... Batt. ⎭	Batterie	battery.
Bay.	Bayerisch	Bavarian.
B.b.a.	Bahnhof-Betriebs-Amt ...	Railway Traffic Office.
Bd. G.	Brand-Geschoss	incendiary shell.
Bd. Z.	Boden-Zünder	base fuze.
Beil.	Beilage	annexe ; enclosure ; appendix.
Bel. Pk.	Belagerungs-Park	siege park.
Bel. Tel. Abt. ...	Belagerungs-Telegraphen-Abteilung	siege telegraph detachment.
Bel. Tr.	Belagerungs-Train	siege train.
Beob. ... ⎧ ⎨ ⎩	Beobachter ... ... Beobachtungs- ...	observer. observation-.
Beob. W. ...	Beobachtungswagen ...	observation wagon.
Besp. Abt. ...	Bespannungs-Abteilung ...	draught horse section.
betr. ...· ⎧ ⎨ ⎩	betreffend ⎫ ⎬ ... ... betreffs ⎭	concerning.
Bez. Offz. ...	Bezirks-Offizier	district officer.
bez. ⎫ ⎬ ... bezüg. ⎭	bezüglich	with reference to.
bezw.	beziehungsweise	or as the case may be.
Bhf.	Bahnhof	railway station (*topog.*)
Bivl.	Beobachter in der vorderen Linie	forward observer.
Bl. ...	blind	blind (*shell*).
Blst.	Block-Station	block signal station (*railway* ; *topog.*).
Br.	Brigade	Brigade.
Br.	Brunnen	well (*topog.*).
Brck. Tr. ...	Brücken-Train	bridging train.
B.R.D.	Bayrische-Reserve-Division ...	Bavarian Reserve Division.
Br. Gef. Std ...	Brigade-Gefechts-Stand ...	Brigade Battle Hqrs.
Brig.	Brigade	Brigade.
Br. Mrs.	Bronze-Mörser	bronze mortar.
Br. Tr.	Brücken-Train	bridging train.
b. St.	beim Stabe	*not translated ; it refers to officers who are attached to regimental H.Q. in peace time.*
B.T.K.	Bereitschafts-Truppen-Kommandeur	commander of the supports.
Btl.	Bataillon	battalion.
Bttr.	Batterie	battery.
B.W.	Bahn-Wärter	plate-layer's hut (*railway* ; *topog.*).
Bz.	Brenn-Zünder	time fuze.

Abbreviation.	Signification.	English Equivalent.

C.

C/92	Construction/92	1892 pattern (*ammn.*).
C.G.S.	Chef des General-Stabes ...	Chief of the General Staff.
Chev. Leg. ...	Chevaulegers	"Chevaulegers" (Bavarian light cavalry).
Ch. Hs.	Chaussee-Haus...	turnpike (*topog.*).
d. B.	durch Bote	by messenger.

D.

D. Br .Tr. ...	Divisions-Brücken-Train ...	Divisional bridging train.
Div.	Division	Division.
d. O.	durch Ordonnanz	by orderly.
Dopp. Z. ...	Doppel-Zünder...	time and percussion fuze.
D.P.	Doppelposten.	double sentry post.
D.R.	Dragoner-Regiment	dragoon regiment.
Dreh. Br. ...	Drehbrücke	swing bridge (*topog.*).
D.T.B.	Divisions-Tages-Befehl ...	Divisional Daily Order.
Dz. ... } D.Z. ...	Doppel-Zünder	time and percussion fuze.

Abbreviation.	Signification.	English Equivalent.

E.

Ec.	Eisen-Centrierung	with rear driving band only (*shell*).
Eis. Tr.	Eisenbahn-Truppen	railway troops.
E.K.Z.	Empfindlicher Kanonen-Zünder	sensitive gun fuze
Ers.	Ersatz	" Ersatz " (*see under* " *Ersatz* ")
Esk.	Eskadron	squadron.
Et.	Etappen	Lines of Communication.
Ex. Pl.	Exerzier-Platz	drill ground (*topog.*).
Exz.	Exzellenz	Excellency (*title given to Lieut.-Generals and senior ranks in the German Army*).

Abbreviation.	Signification.	English Equivalent.

F.

F. ...	Feind	the enemy.
	feindlich	hostile, the enemy's.
(F)	Feld-Haubitze	*indicates a light field howitzer battery, ammunition column, &c.*
f.	für	for.
F.A.	Feld-Artillerie	field artillery.
F.A.B.	Feld-Artillerie-Brigade ...	field artillery brigade.
F.A.Btl.	Fuss-Artillerie-Bataillon ...	foot artillery battalion.
F.A.R.	Feld-Artillerie-Regiment ...	field artillery regiment.
Fb.	Fliehbolzen	centrifugal bolt (*in fuze, etc.*).
Fbba.	Feld-Bahn-Betriebs-Amt ...	field railway traffic office.
Fbr.	Fabrik	factory (*topog.*).
f.Bttr. ...	fahrende Batterie ...	field artillery battery.
fdl.	feindlich	hostile, the enemy's.
Fd. Laz. ...	Feld-Lazarett	field hospital.
f.d.R. ...	für die Richtigkeit ...	certified correct.
Fe.	Fernsprech-Abteilung ...	telephone detachment.
feindl. ...	feindlich	hostile, the enemy's.
Felda. ...	Feld-Artillerie	field artillery.
Feldlaz. ...	Feld-Lazarett	field hospital.
Feldw. ...	Feldwebel	serjeant-major.
Fernsp. Abt. ...	Fernsprech-Abteilung ...	telephone detachment.
Fest.	Festung (s-)	fortress.
F.Fr. ...	Feindliche Flammenwerfer ...	hostile *Flammenwerfer.*
F.Gr.	Feld-Granate	field gun high explosive (H.E.) shell.
F.H.	Feld-Haubitze	light field howitzer.
F.K.	Feld-Kanone	field gun.
F.L.	Feld-Lazarett	field hospital.
Fl.	Fluss	river (*topog*).
Flak.	Flug-Abwehr-Kanone ...	anti-aircraft gun.
Flakgmko ...	Flug - Abwehr - Kanonen - Gruppen - Kommandeur	A. A. Group Commander.
Flak-Zug... ...	Flug-Abwehr-Kanonen-Zug	anti-aircraft section.
Fldart.	Feld-Artillerie	field artillery.
Fldbäck. K. ...	Feld-Bäckerei-Kolonne ...	field bakery column.
Fldverw. Beh. ...	Feldverwaltungs-Behörden ...	field administrative authorities.
Fliehb ...	Fliehbolzen	centrifugal bolt (*in fuze, etc.*).
F. M.G. F. ...	feindliches Maschinen-Gewehr Feuer.	hostile machine gun fire.
F.M.G.Z.... ...	Feld-Maschinen-Gewehr-Zug...	machine gun section.
F.O.	Felddienst-Ordnung	Field Service Regulations.
F. Patr.	Feld-Patrone	field gun cartridge (*fixed ammunition*).
Fp.	Fuhrpark	transport park.
F.P. Amt. ⎫ F.P.A. ⎭ ...	Feld-Post-Amt.	field post office.
Fp. 02	Füllpulver 02	1902 pattern explosive (T.N.T.)
Fp. D.O. ...	Feldpost-Dienst-Ordnung ...	Regulations for the Field Postal Service.

Abbreviation.	Signification.	English Equivalent.
F. Pi. D. ...	Feld-Pionier-Dienst (aller Waffen)	Manual of Field Engineering for All Arms.
F.P. Exp. } F.P. E. } ...	Feld-Post-Expedition... ...	branch field post office.
Fp. K. } Fpk. K. } ...	Fuhr-Park-Kolonne ...	supply park.
F. P. St. } F. P. S. } ...	Feld-Post-Station ...	field post office.
franz.	französisch	French.
Fr. Wag.... ...	Futterwagen	forage wagon.
F.S.	Feld-Schmiede ...	field forge.
F. Sp.	feindliches Sperrfeuer	hostile barrage fire.
Fsp. } F. Spr. } ...	Fernsprech (er)	telephone.
Ft.	Funken-Telegraphie ...	wireless telegraphy (W/T).
Ft. Sperre ...	Funken-Telegraphie-Sperre !...	Stop using wireless !
Fu	Funker	wireless.
Fufa	Funker-Feld-Abteilung ...	field wireless detachment.
Fukla	Funker-Klein-Abteilung ...	trench wireless detachment.
Füs.	Füsilier	fusilier.
Fuss-A. } Fussart. } ...	Fuss-Artillerie	foot artillery.
Fuss. A.R. ...	Fuss-Artillerie-Regiment ...	foot artillery regiment.
Fuss. A.B. ...	Fuss-Artillerie-Bataillon ...	foot artillery battalion.
F.V.T.	Feld-Verpflegungs-Tabellen ...	Field Supply Tables.
F.W.	Futterwagen	forage wagon.
F. W. St. ...	Feld-Wetter-Station	meteorological station.
f.10 cm. K. ...	für 10 cm. Kanone	for 10 -cm. gun.

G.

G.	Granate...	high explosive (H.E.) shell.
g.	geheim	secret.
Gd.	Garde	Guard.
Gef. Ordnz ...	Gefechts-Ordonnanz ...	orderly, runner.

Abbreviation.	Signification.	English Equivalent.
Gefr.	Gefreiter	lance-corporal.
Gef. Std. ...	Gefechts-Stand	battle headquarters.
geh.	geheim	secret.
gel.	geladen	loaded.
gem. ... {	gemäss	according to.
	gemischt	mixed.
Gen. d. Pion. ...	General der Pioniere ...	Pioneer General.
Gen. Kdo.(s) } Genkdo(s) }	General-Kommando(s) ...	Staff of an Army Corps, Corps Headquarters.
Gesch. ... {	Geschütz	gun.
	Geschoss	projectile.
gez. ... {	gezeichnet	signed.
	gezogen	rifled.
Gf. ... {	Geschütz-Fabrik	gun factory.
	Geschoss-Fabrik	shell factory.
G.g.	Granate-Geschoss ...	high explosive (H.E.) shell.
Gkofunk	General-Kommando - Funker-Kommando	Corps Wireless H.Q.
gl. l. W.M. Lanz	glatte leichte Wurf-Mine Lanz	light smooth bore Lanz *Minenwerfer* H.E. shell.
Gouv.	Gouvernement	Government.
G.R.	Grenadier-Regiment ...	grenadier regiment.
Gr.	Granate...	high explosive (H.E.) shell.
Gr.	Gross (-er, -e, -es)	great.
Gr. Bag. ...	Grosse Bagage	baggage section of the train.
Grf. 88 ...	Granatfüllung 88	1888 pattern explosive (picric acid).
Gr. Gen. Stab ...	Grosser General-Stab.... ...	Great General Staff.
Gr. H. Qu. ...	Grosses Hauptquartier ...	General Headquarters.
Gr. H. Qu. ...	Gruppen-Hauptquartier ...	Army Group Headquarters.
Groftrupp ...	Grosser-Flammenwerfèr-Trupp	large *Flammenwerfer* squad.
Gr. Z.	Granat-Zünder...	fuze for HE.. shell.
G.R.z.F.	Garde-Regiment zu Fuss. ...	Foot Guards regiment.
G.S.O.	Gas-Schutz-Offizier	anti-gas officer.
G.S.U.	Gas-Schutz-Unteroffizier ...	anti-gas N.C.O.
Gtt. Br.	Gitter-Brücke	lattice girder bridge (*topog.*).
Gv.	Garnisonsverwendungsfähig ...	suitable for garrison employment.
G.V.E.	Garnisonsverwendungsfähig im Etappen gebiet.	fit for duty on the L. of C.
G.V.F.	Garnisonsverwendungsfähig im Felde.	fit for duty with regimental transport, &c.
G.V.H.	Garnisonsverwendungsfähig in der Heimat.	fit for garrison duty in Germany.

Abbreviation.	Signification.	English Equivalent.

H.

H.	Haubitze	howitzer.
Hauptm. ...	Hauptmann	Captain.
H.Gr.	Haubitz-Granate	howitzer H.E. shell.
Hp.	Halte-Punkt	stopping place (*railway*; *topog.*).
Hptm.	Hauptmann	Captain.
H.R.	Husaren-Regiment	hussar regiment.
Hus.	Husaren	hussars.
H.Z.	Haubitz-Zünder	howitzer fuze.

I.

i.A.	im Auftrag	" By order," "Signed for " (*above a signature on a document*).
I.B.	Infanterie-Brigade	Infantry Brigade.
I.D.	Infanterie-Division	Infantry Division.
i. Kas. L.	in Kasematten-Lafette ...	on casemate mounting.
i. Kst. L	in Küsten-Lafette	on coast defence mounting.
I.M.K. ...	Infanterie-Munitions-Kolonne	infantry ammunition column.
Intdr. ...	Intendantur	Intendance.
i. P.L.	in Panzer-Lafette	on shielded mounting.
J.R.	Infanterie-Regiment	infantry regiment.
i.S.I.	in Schirm-Lafette	on carriage with overhead shield.
i.V.	in Vertretung	" By order," "Signed for " (*above a signature on a document*).
Iz.	Innen-Zünder	internal fuze.

Abbreviation.	Signification.	English Equivalent.

J.

J.B.	Jäger-Bataillon	"Jäger" battalion.
J.R.	Infanterie-Regiment	infantry regiment.

K.

K.	Kanone	gun.
K.	Kartätsche	case shot.
K.	Kolonne	column.
K.	Kompagnie	company.
K.	Korps	Corps.
k.	kürzer	shorter.
Kagol.	Kampfflugzeug - Geschwader, Oberste Heeresleitung.	Battle-plane Squadron under General Headquarters.
Kan. ... {	Kanone	gun.
	Kanonier	gunner.
Kart.	Kartusche	cartridge (gun or howitzer ; it implies that it is not fixed ammunition).
Kav. Div. ...	Kavallerie-Division ...	Cavalry Division.
K.B.	Königlich-Bayerisch. ...	Royal Bavarian.
K.D.	Kaiserlich-Deutsch ...	Imperial German.
K.D.	Kavallerie-Division	Cavalry Division.

Abbreviation.	Signification.	English Equivalent.
Kd. d. Krftftr. ...	Kommandeur der Kraftfahr-Truppen.	Commander of the Motor Transport Troops.
Kdo.	Kommando	command, word of command; party, detachment.
Kdr.	Kommandeur	Commander.
Kdt. H. Qu. ⎱ K.d.H.Qu. ⎰	Kommandant des Haupt-quartiers.	Camp Commandant.
Kdtr. ...	Kommandantur	Commandant's office.
K.F.	Kahnfähre	ferry by rowing boat (topog.).
K.F.	Kompagnie-Führer	company commander (on trench maps, &c.).
K.f.b.Z.	Kriegsverwendungsfähig fur besondere Zwecke.	fit for active service in certain capacities. (sometimes used of men classed in category "Garnisonsver-wendungsfähig ").
K.G.O.H.L. ...	Kampfflugzeug-Geschwader, Oberste-Heeresleitung.	Battle-plane Squadron under General Headquarters.
K. Gr.	Kanonen-Granate	gun-shell.
Khf.	Kirchhof	churchyard (topog.).
K.H.Qu.	Korps-Hauptquartier... ...	Corps Headquarters.
K.i.H.	Kanone in Haubitzlafette ...	" K.i.H." field gun (new pattern 7·7-cm. field gun on howitzer carriage).
Kino.	Kinematograph	Cinematograph.
Kl.	Klein	small.
Kleiftrupp ...	Kleiner-Flammenwerfer-Trupp	small Flammenwerfer squad.
Kl.F.w.	Kleiner Flammenwerfer ...	small Flammenwerfer.
K. Ltg.	Kabel-Leitung	cable line.
K-Munition ...		" K-ammunition " (armour-piercing ammunition, for rifle) or K-shell (asphyxiating gas shell).
K.M., Z.Ch. ...	Zentralstelle für Fragen der Chemie im Kriegs-Minis-terium.	Central Office for Chemical Questions in the Ministry of War.
Kofe.	Kommandeur der Fernsprech-truppen.	Commander of Telephon·· Troops (at Army H.Q.).
Kofl. ⎱ Koflieg. ⎰ ...	Kommandeur der Flieger-Truppen.	Commander of Aviation Troops (with Corps, &c.).
Koflak.	Kommandeur der Flug-Abwehr Kanonen.	Commander of the Anti-aircraft Guns.
Kofu. ⎱ Kofunk. ⎰ ...	Kommandeur der Funker-truppen.	Commander of Wireless Troops (at Army H.Q.).
Kogen-Luft. ...	Kommandierender General der Luftstreitkräfte.	Commander of the Air Forces.
Kol.	Kolonne	column.
Komp.	Kompagnie	company.
Korp.	Korporalschaft	section (¼ of a " Zug ").
Kplschaft. ...	Korporalschaft	section (¼ of a " Zug ").
K.Pr.	Königlich-Preussisch ...	Royal Prussian.
Kr. (in a post-mark)	Kreis	district.
Kr M.	Kriegs-Ministerium	War Ministry.
Krak. W. ...	Krankenwagen...	ambulance wagon.
K.S.	Königlich-Sächsisch	Royal Saxon.

Abbreviation.	Signification.	English Equivalent.
K. Sig. 16 ...	Kleine Signal-Gerät 16 ...	Small 1916 pattern signalling apparatus.
K.S.O.	Kriegssanitätsordnung ...	Field Medical Regulations.
Kst.	Küste (n)	coast (coast defence).
Kst. H. ...	Küsten-Haubitze	coast defence howitzer.
Kst. K. ...	Küsten-Kanone	coast defence gun.
Kst. Mrs. ...	Küsten-Mörser	coast defence mortar.
k.s.W.M. ...	kurze schwere Wurf-Mine ...	heavy *Minenwerfer* short H.E. shell.
Kt.	Kartätsche	case shot.
K.T.A.	Korps-Telegraphen-Abteilung	Corps telegraph detachment.
K.T.B.	Korps-Tages-Befehl	Corps Daily Order.
K.T.K.	Kampf - Truppen - Kommandeur.	Commander of the front line troops.
Kt.O.	Krankenträger-Ordnung ...	Stretcher Bearer Regulations.
Ktt. Br	Kettenbrücke	suspension bridge (*topog.*).
Kür. R. ...	Kürassier-Regiment ...	Cuirassier regiment.
K.V.	Kriegsverwendungsfähig ...	fit for active service.
K.V.V. ...	Kriegs-Verpflegungs-Vorschrift.	Field Supply Regulations.
K.W	Königlich-Württembergisch ...	Royal Württemberg.
K.Z.	Kanonen-Zünder	gun fuze.
Kz. ...	Kopf-Zünder	nose fuze.
K. Zug. ...	Kanonenmunitions-Zug ...	gun ammunition train.
Kz. Bd. Z. ...	Kurzer Boden-Zünder ...	short base fuze.

L.

L.	Lafette	gun carriage, mounting.
L.	Lang	long.
L.	Länger	longer.
L.	Leicht	light.
Ladekdo ...	Lade-Kommando	battery charging detachment (*wireless*).
Landw. ...	Landwehr	Landwehr (*not translated*).

Abbreviation.	Signification.	English Equivalent.
Laz.	Lazarett	hospital.
l.B.	lange Brennlänge	long burning (fuze).
Ldst.	Landsturm	Landsturm (not translated).
Ldstm.	Landsturmmann	man of the Landsturm.
Ldw.	Landwehr	Landwehr (not translated).
L.E.		"L.E." (a type of explosive bullet, see under "Munition").
Lebm. K. ...	Lebensmittelkisten	ration boxes.
Lebm. W. ...	Lebensmittelwagen	supply wagon.
l.F.H.	leichte Feld-Haubitze... ...	light field howitzer.
Lg. Bd. Z. ...	Langer Boden-Zünder ...	long base fuze.
lg. Brlg. ...	lange Brennlänge	long burning (fuze).
l. gez.	leichte gezogene	light rifled.
l. gez. W.M. ...	leichte gezogene Wurfmine ...	light rifled Minenwerfer H.E. shell.
Lggr.	Langgranate	long shell.
l.M.G.Tr.... ...	leichter Maschinen-Gewehr-Trupp.	light machine gun section.
l.M.K.	leichte Munitions-Kolonne ...	light ammunition column.
Lst.	Ladestelle	entraining station, loading platform (topog.).
l.s.W.M.	lange schwere Wurf-Mine ...	heavy Minenwerfer long H.E. shell.
Ltn.	Leutnant	2nd Lieutenant.
L.V.	Lautverstärker...	amplifier valve.
L.V.G.	Luft-Verkehrs-Gesellschaft ...	A firm which manufactures aeroplanes known as L.V.G.
l.W.M.	leichte Wurf-Mine	light Minenwerfer H.E. shell.
l.W.M.Zdr. ...	leichter Wurf-Mine-Zünder ...	fuze of light Minenwerfer.
L/3.1, &c. ...	... ...	Used in the nomenclature of projectiles to indicate that the length is 3·1, &c., calibres.
L/4.0, &c. ...	... ...	Used in nomenclature of guns to indicate that the length is 40, &c., calibres.

Abbreviation.	Signification.	English Equivalent.

M.

Abbreviation.	Signification.	English Equivalent.
M.	Mühle	mill (*topog*).
Mdlchb.	Mundlochbüchse	old pattern type of fuze.
Mdlchf.	Mundlochfutter	gaine (*of fuze*).
Mebu.	Maschinengewehr-Eisen-Beton-Unterstand.	reinforced concrete machine-gun emplacement.
M.E.D.	Militär-Eisenbahn-Direktion	Directorate of Military Railways.
M.G.A. } M.G.Abt. } ...	Maschinen-Gewehr-Abteilung	machine gun detachment.
m. gez.	mittlere gezogene	medium rifled.
M.G.K. } M.G.Kp. } ...	Maschinen-Gewohr-Kompagnie	machine gun company.
m. gl.	mittlere glatte	medium smooth bore.
M.G.S.s.K. ...	Maschinen-Gewehr-Scharf-schützen-Kompagnie.	machine gun marksman company.
M.G.S.s.T. ...	Maschinen-Gewehr-Scharf-schützen-Trupp.	machine gun marksman section
M.H. ...	Minen-Hülle ... ·	canister bomb.
Mil.-Url.-Zug. ...	Militär-Urlaubs-Zug	military leave train.
Min.	Mine (n)	mine or *Minenwerfer* shell.
Min.	Mineur (Kompagnie)	mining company.
Mi. W. K.	Minenwerfer-Kompagnie ...	trench mortar company.
M.K.	Munitions-Kolonne	ammunition column.
Mk.	Marschkolonne...	column on the march.
m.K.	mit Kappe	with cap (*shell or fuze*).
m.M.W.	mittlerer Minenwerfer... ...	medium *Minenwerfer*.
m. Ozdg	mit Oberzündung	with overhead ignition (*pattern of 21 cm. mortar*).
Mrs.	Mörser	(21 cm.) mortar.
Mrs. Battr. ...	Mörser-Batterie	(21 cm.) mortar battery.
M.S.	Melde-Sammelstelle	report centre.
M. Sig. 16 ...	Mittlere Signal-Gerät 16 ...	medium 1916 pattern sig. nalling apparatus.
Mtl. K.	Mantel-Kanone	jacketed gun.
Mun.	Munition	ammunition.
M.V.	Mit Verzögerung	with delay action (*fuze*).
M.W.	Minenwerfer	*Minenwerfer* (*trench mortar*).
M.W.	Munitionswagen	ammunition wagon.
m.W.M.	mittlere Wurf-Mine	medium *Minenwerfer* H.E. shell.

Abbreviation.	Signification.	English Equivalent.

N.

n.	nach	" to " (*direction of road*).
n.	nördlich	north of, northerly.
n/A.	neuer Art	new pattern.
nachm.	nachmittags	in the afternoon, p.m.
nördl.	nördlich	north of, northerly.
N.M.O.	Nachrichten-Mittel-Offizier ...	communication officer.
N.O.	Nachrichten-Offizier	intelligence officer.

O.

o.	östlich	east of, easterly.
O.A.	Offizier-Aspirant	probationary or aspirant officer.
O./A. (*in a postmark*).	Ober-Amt.	Head Office (*postal*).
Offz.	Offizier	officer.
Off. Stellv. ...	Offizier-Stellvertreter	acting officer (*but usually not translated*).
O-Punkt ...	Null-Punkt	aiming point, reference point.
O.Q.	Oberquartiermeister	*see page 88.*
östl.	östlich	east of, easterly.
O.U.	Orts-Unterkunft	(*ordinary*) billets.
O.V.	Ohne Verzögerung	without delay action, direct action (*fuze*).

Abbreviation.	Signification.	English Equivalent.

P.

P.	Pulver	powder (*usually black powder*).
Patr.	Patrone	cartridge (*in the case of a gun, only when it is fixed ammunition*).
Patr. W. ...	Patronenwagen	small arms ammunition wagon.
Pf. D.	Pferdedepot	remount depôt.
Pi.) B., Kp., &c.) Pion(B. Kp., &c.).	Pionier (-Bataillon,● Kompagnie, &c.)	pioneer (battalion, company, &c.).
Pk. W.	Packwagen	baggage wagon.
Pl. W.	Planwagen	ladder-sided wagon.
p.p.	*praemissis praemittendis* ...	&c., &c.
Prov.	Proviant	supply.
Prov. Amt. ...	Proviant-Amt	supply depôt.
Pr. K.	Proviant-Kolonne	supply column.

Q.

| Q.M. ... ... | Quadratmeter ... ... | square metre. |

Abbreviation.	Signification.	English Equivalent.

R.

R.	Regiment	regiment.
r.	reitende...	horse (*e.g., artillery*).
Radf.	Radfahrer	cyclist.
R.A.K.	Reserve-Armee-Korps ...	Reserve (Army) Corps.
r. Bttr.	reitende Batterie	horse artillery battery.
Res.	Reserve	reserve.
Rev. K.	Revolver-Kanone ...	revolver-gun.
R.I.R.	Reserve-Infanterie-Regiment	reserve infantry regiment.
Rittm.	Rittmeister ... ● ...	Captain (*of cavalry or train*).
R.K.	Ring-Kanone	gun with chase rings.

S.

S.	Schrapnell	shrapnel.
s.	schwer	heavy.
s.	südlich	south of, southerly.
s.	siehe	see, *vide*.
s.A.d. Feldh. ...	schwere Artillerie des Feld-heeres.	Heavy Artillery of the Field Army.
San.	Sanitäts-	medical.
San. K. ...	} Sanitäts-Kompagnie	medical *or* bearer company.
San. Kp....		
S.B.	Soldatenbrief	soldier's letter.
Sch.	Scheune	barn (*topog.*).
Sch.	Schrapnell	shrapnel.
Schä*f*.	Schäferei	sheep farm (*topog.*).
Scheinw. Zg. ...	Scheinwerferzug	searchlight section.
Schr.	Schrapnell	shrapnel.
Schw. R.R. ...	Schweres Reiter-Regiment ...	heavy cavalry regiment (*Bavarian or Saxon.*)
Sek.	Sekunden	seconds.
Sekt.	Sektion	section.
Selbst.	selbständig	independent.

Abbreviation.	Signification.	English Equivalent.
s.F.H.	schwere Feld-Haubitze ...	heavy field howitzer.
s.F.H. 02 (&c.) ...	schwere Feld-Haubitze ...	1902 (&c.) pattern heavy field howitzer.
s.F.St.	schwere Funkenstation ...	heavy wireless station.
S-Munition ...		" S " ammunition (*see under " Munition*").
Sprgr. ...	Spreng-Granate	high explosive (H.E.) shell.
S.S. Trupp ...	Scharfschützen-Trupp ...	(machine gun) marksman section.
Stbr.	Steinbruch	quarry (*topog*.).
St.	Stab	staff, H.Q.
St.	Stellung	position.
Stellv.	Stellvertretend...	acting, deputy.
Stofelda	Stabs-Offizier der Feld Artillerie	Staff Officer for Field Artillery.
Stofl.	Stabsoffizier der Flieger-Truppen	Staff Officer for Aviation (*at Army H.Q.*).
St.O.Gas ...	Stabs-Offizier für Gas ...	Army Gas Officer.
Stoluft	Stabs-Offizier der Luftschiffer-Truppen	Staff Officer for Air Services.
St.O.M.G. ...	Stabs-Offizier für Maschinen-Gewehre.	Staff Officer for Machine Guns.
Stoverm.... ...	Stabs-Officier der Vermessungs-Abteilung	Staff Officer for Survey.
St. Qu.	Stabsquartier	Headquarters.
südl.	südlich	south of, southerly.
s.W.M.	schwere Wurf-Mine	heavy *Minenwerfer* H.E. shell.

T.

t.	Tonne	metric ton (2,205 *lbs.*).
Tel.	Telegraph	telegraph.
Tel. Abt. Telegr. Abt. }	Telegraphen-Abteilung ...	telegraph detachment.
T.H.	Turm-Haubitze	howitzer in turret.

Abbreviation.	Signification.	English Equivalent.
T.K.	Turm-Kanone	gun in turret.
T-Munition ...		T-shell (*lachrymatory gas shell*).
Tr.	Train	Train (*not translated*).
Tr.	Trupp	section, party, squad.
transf.	transformiert	converted (*ammunition*).
Trig. P. ...	Trigonometrischer Punkt ...	trigonometrical point (*topog.*)
Tr. Üb. Pl. ...	Truppen-Übungs-Platz ...	training ground.

U.

U.	Unterrichts-	instructional.
u.	und	and.
u.	urschriftlich	autographic, in original.
U.A.K.	Unter-Abschnitts-Kommand- eur.	sub-sector commander.
Üb.	Übungs-	practice.
überw.	überwiesen	allotted.
Übgr.	Übungsgranate	practice shell.
Üb. Ldg ...	Übungs-Ladung	practice charge.
Üb, Pl.	Übungs-Platz	training ground.
Ul.	Ulan	" Ulan " (*lancer*).
Ul. R.	Ulanen-Regiment ...	" Ulanen " regiment (*lancer regiment*).
umg. ...	{ umgeändert umgearbeitet }	converted (*ammunition*).
U. St.	Unterstand	dug-out.
Uffz. } U. Offz. }	Unteroffizier	non-commissioned officer : *also* " under-officer," *which is a special rank of N.C.O. corresponding to our corporal.*
u.U.	unter Umständen	according to circumstances ; in certain circumstances.

Abbreviation.	Signification.	English Equivalent.
	V.	
v.	von	"from" (*direction of road*).
V.d.F.H. ...	Verpflegung des Feldheeres ...	supply of the Field Army.
Verm. Abtlg. ...	Vermessungs-Abteilung ...	survey section
Verpfl.	Verpflegung	supply (*food*).
verst.	verstärkt	strengthened.
V.G.U.	verlesen, genehmigt, unter- schrieben.	noted, approved, signed.
v.H.	von Hundert	per cent.
V.K.	Verkürzte Kammerhülse ...	shortened central tube (*of shrapnel*).
V.K.	Vorposten-Kompagnie ...	outpost company.
V.L.	Vereins-Lazarett ...	auxiliary hospital.
V.O.	Verbindungs-Offizier	liaison officer.
vorm.	vormittags	in the morning, a.m.
Vorst. ⎫ Vrst. ⎬ ... ... Vst. ⎭	Vorstecker	safety pin (*of fuze*).
V.S.d. ...	Von Seiten des...	for .... (*above signature*).
V.W.	Vorrats-Wagen	store wagon.
Vw.	Vorwerk	farm, manor (*topog*).
Vz. Wm. ...	Vizewachtmeister	vice-serjeant-major (*mounted troops*).

Abbreviation.	Signification.	English Equivalent.
	W.	
w.... ⎫ westl. ⎭	westlich...	west of, westerly.
	westlich...	west of, westerly.
W.F.	Wagen-Fähre	ferry for wagons (*topog.*).
W.M.	Wurf-Mine	*Minenwerfer* H.E. shell.
Wth.	Wacht-Turm	watch tower (*topog*).
W.U.	Wohn-Unterstand ...	living dug-out.
Wumba	Waffen und Munitions-Be- schaffungs-Amt	Munitions Department of the War Ministry.
	Z.	
Z.	Zünder	fuze.
Z.A.B. ...	Zivil-Arbeiter-Bataillon ...	civilian labour battalion.
z.B.	zum Beispiel	for example.
z.D.	zur Disposition	on half pay (*of officers*).
Zdg.	Zündung	fuze.
Zdldg. ⎫ Zdlg. ⎭ ...	Zündladung	exploder (*in a shell*).
Zdr.	Zünder	fuze, detonator.
z. F.	zu Fuss	Foot (*Guards*).
Zgl.	Ziegelei	brick-field (*topog.*).
Ziff.	Ziffer	paragraph; cipher; numeral.
Z.m.W.M. ...	Zünder mittlerer Wurf-Mine ...	fuze of medium *Minenwerfer*.
Z-Schlüssel ...	Zünder-Schlüssel	fuze key.
Z.s.W.M.... ...	Zünder schwerer Wurf-Mine ...	fuze of heavy *Minenwerfer*.
Z.s.u.m.W.M. ...	Zünder schwerer und mittlerer Wurf-Mine.	fuze of heavy and medium *Minenwerfer*.
z.T.	zum Teil	partly.
zuget. ...	zugeteilt	allotted to.
z.Z.	zur Zeit	at present.

Abbreviations not ordinarily found in documents, but sometimes employed in telephone and wireless messages.

Abbreviation.	Signification.	English Equivalent.
DLT.	Drahtlose Telegraphie ...	wireless telegraphy.
DR.	Drahtverhau	" wire," wire entanglement.
EB. ·	erbeten	requested.
E....	Eigene Truppen	our troops.
EA.	Eigene Artillerie	our artillery.
EDG.	Etat der Gewehrmunition ...	statement showing quantity of rifle ammunition available.
EF.	erforderlichen Falls	if necessary.
EFR.	Eigenes Flammenwerfer ...	our *Flammenwerfer*.
EGMIN.	Eigenes Gasminenfeuer ...	our *Minenwerfer* gas shell fire.
EI.	Eigene Infanterie	our infantry.
EI.—VW. ...	EigeneInfanterie geht vorwärts	our infantry is advancing.
EMG.	Eigenes M.G. Feuer	our machine gun fire.
EMIN.	Eigenes Minenfeuer	our *Minenwerfer* fire.
ESP.	Eigenes Sperrfeuer	our barrage fire.
FA.	feindiche Artillerie	hostile artillery.
FGMIN.	feindliches Gasminenfeuer ...	hostile *Minenwerfer* gas shell fire.
FI.	feindliche Infanterie	hostile infantry.
FMIN.	feindliches Minenfeuer ...	hostile *Minenwerfer* fire.
GGR.	Gasgranate	gas shell.
GMIN.	Gas-Mine	*Minenwerfer* gas shell.
GT.	Granate	high explosive (H.E.) shell.
GW.	Gerätewagen	pioneer store wagon.
GW.	Granat-Zünder...	fuze for H.E. shell.
GZ.	Geschütz	gun.
HB.	Haubitzbatterie	howitzer battery.
HDGR. VW. ...	Handgranaten vorwärts ! ...	Bring up hand grenades !
I. MUN. VW. ...	Infanterie-Munition vorwärts !	Bring up small arms ammunition !
KODR	Kommandantur	Commandant's office
LW	Lebensmittelwagen	supply wagon.
M.	Trommelfeuer	intense bombardment.
MIN. VW. ...	Minen vorwärts !	Bring up trench mortar ammunition !
M Q	Marschquartier	billet on the line of march.
OB.	Orts-Biwak	close billets.
OQ.	Orts-Quartier	billet.
PW.	Packwagen	baggage wagon.

Abbreviation.	Signification.	English Equivalent.
RP.	Relaisposten	relay posts.
SA.	Schwere Artillerie	heavy artillery.
SA.	Sandsäcke	sand bags.
SKO.	Sanitätskompagnie	medical *or* bearer company.
TZ.	Tagesziel	day target, target of the day (?)
ZP.	Zielpunkt	objective.
ZP. NR-G. ...	Zielpunkt Nr.—gefangen ...	Objective No. — captured.